THE ULTIMATE AUDITION BOOK
VOLUME 5

222 MORE COMEDY MONOLOGUES
2 MINUTES AND UNDER

The Ultimate Audition Book
Volume 5

222 MORE Comedy Monologues
2 Minutes and Under

Edited by
Irene Ziegler and John Capecci

Smith and Kraus   2017

ISBN: 9781575259116
Library of Congress Control Number: 2017932527

Typesetting and layout design by Elizabeth E. Monteleone
Cover by Aimee Libby

A Smith and Kraus book
177 Lyme Road, Hanover, NH 03755
Editorial 603.643.6431 Orders 1.877.668.8680
www.smithandkraus.com

Printed in the United States of America

*For the very funny family, friends and colleagues we miss
dearly and who continue to make us smile, especially
Gianna Capecci
Ronald E. Ziegler
Ric Roe
David Rakoff and Spalding Gray*

CONTENTS

Male Comic Monologues

FEMALE SERIOCOMIC MONOLOGUES

MALE SERIOCOMIC MONOLOGUES

GENDER-NEUTRAL MONOLOGUES

INDICES

INTRODUCTION

If you've ever searched for a good comic monologue—whether for a professional audition, a class or a competition—you know how frustrating the hunt can be. To rephrase the old theater adage (attributed to actor Edmund Kean, among others): Dying is easy; finding comic monologues is hard.

Well, you can stop rifling through those other monologue books and websites (with the exception of our first collection of 222 comic monologues, which was a corker), looking for the rare selection that doesn't begin with "I have two weeks to live," "There's something you should know" or "You ungrateful bastard." We've combed through some of the world's best comic writing—and sacrificed another good year of our lives—to bring you *222 MORE Comedy Monologues: Two Minutes and Under.* It's all funny stuff here: contemporary works and a few classics, roles for men and women young and old, and entertaining voices from writers as varied as Anton Chekhov, Will Eno, Clare Booth Luce, David Rakoff, Mark Twain and Katy Wix. Many of the authors represented here appear in print for the first time, and we're delighted to give them this opportunity.

In our continuing effort to offer you new sources of monologues, we've drawn from plays, original freestanding monologues, short stories, essays, blogs and memoirs. You'll find shades of comedy from light to dark: situational humor, word play, absurdity, surrealism. These monologues are alternately romantic, silly, nasty, downright zany—first-rate character work by some very funny people.

What is a Comic Monologue?

In *The Ultimate Audition Series*, we define a monologue as "a short, self-contained work or excerpt that features a central speaker and contains some change in thought, emotion or action." Comic monologues are the ones that fit that description...and also are funny.

You may not feel that all the monologues here *are* funny; that's fine. Humor is personal. And that's about as far as we'll go into the psychological examination of comedy. Sometimes a banana peel is just a banana peel.

But we will say this: not all humorous writing makes for a good performance monologue. In a good monologue, the words arise from or hint at the context. Without some sense of the character's world (someone saying something funny, somewhere), the performer isn't given much to sink his or her oversized wax teeth into. So, the selections we've included in this collection all contain a good dose of character and attitude. It's the performer's challenge to fill in the gaps and put flesh on the funny bones.

We probably don't need to mention this, but we will anyway: to fully understand and ultimately embody the characters in this book, seek out and read the monologue's original source. Most of these characters exist beyond the pages of this collection, and you need to explore the greater context to answer these all-important questions: who, what, when, where and why? Check the permissions page for information on where to find the original works, Google™ the playwrights, visit Doollee.com or check your local library.

So, What's a Seriocomic Monologue?

Put simply: Comic monologues go for the gut; seriocomic monologues aim a little higher and to the right.

A comic monologue is, first and foremost, intentionally funny. But a seriocomic monologue uses humor to express, or sometimes mask, a more serious intent. The seriocomic monologue shows characters laughing through their tears (*The Norwegians,* by C. Denby Swanson), employing humor to address important issues (*God Only Knows,* by Michael Bailey) or metaphorically slicing their enemies with saber wit (*7th Period Lunch, or Someone's Gonna Snap,* by David Don Miller).

The seriocomic monologue offers the performer the opportunity to strike that delicate balance between comedy and drama. And like most good monologues, seriocomics have, at some point, a turn in thought, emotion or action. Often, that turn is found in the shift from the comedic to the dramatic—the monologue's equivalent of "but, seriously, folks..."

How to Use This Book

At the back of this volume, you'll find all 222 monologues neatly arranged and cleverly indexed by age/gender, author and classic/contemporary.

Age is noted exactly only when specified by the author. More often, we've indicated a range (20s, 20s-30s). In some instances, we've used a plus sign to show the character could be older than indicated (40+).

Classic/contemporary refers to when the monologue was written, not necessarily when the character is speaking. Classic texts are those that were written prior to the early 1920s.

Freestanding monologue refers to a monologue that was written as such, and is not taken from a larger work, such as a play or essay. We made this distinction for classroom use; for monologues lifted from larger works, be sure to read the originals for additional insights into character and context.

Whenever possible, we've attempted to excerpt monologues with a minimum of editing. Where editing was necessary, omissions are indicated by parenthetical ellipses (…). All other ellipses were part of the original texts.

Why is it Difficult to Find a Good, Brief, Comic Monologue?

Partly because comic performance is more often based in the act; dramatic performance is more often based in the telling. In other words: if you take away a character's funny walk, stage business, double-takes, pratfalls and props, you have precious few words left. So, it's tough to find a good comic character speech that sustains for a full two minutes. But we suspect it all boils down to a Kean observation: Comedy is hard.

Irene Ziegler and John Capecci

FEMALE
COMIC MONOLOGUES

After (#1)

Chad Beckim

> Play
> Female
> Early 30s
> Comic

Susie, a young Asian woman, notices Monty staring at toothbrushes in a pharmacy. She doesn't realize that after spending many years in prison, he has recently been exonerated for a crime he didn't commit. She helps him choose a toothbrush, then feels bad for being...well, Susie.

SUSIE:

I do this all the time—it's a bad habit and I do it and I'm trying not to do it anymore but it's sort of ingrained, like this horrible part of my personality, I guess, but. Yeah. I'm sorry. (…)

I saw you and wanted to be helpful and instead of being helpful and letting you choose the toothbrush, I came over and inserted myself and asserted myself and made an ass of myself. I've been told that I have problems with that. I've been told that I often confuse being helpful with being assertive.

You're not one of those "Axe" guys, are you? You know— pssssshhhhhhhhhhhtttttttt! (*She "sprays" herself. Monty stares.*) You've never seen it? "Axe?" It's this horribly smelly shit that for some reason guys think smells good and spray all over themselves.

I don't get that, you know? Like, you'll see these good-looking guys, well-groomed, well-maintained, together, the kind of guys that you see and secretly think, "He looks like a nice guy to talk to," only then they walk past you and they smell like they just got stuck in a cologne thunderstorm. You're Latino, right? … And you don't stink like that. You smell natural. Like soap or something. Which is good. So what's up with that? I only ask because it actually made me stop dating black and Latin guys. Which sucks, because I actually prefer black and Latin guys. White guys are too boring and Asian guys all have mom issues. And Jews. (*She hangs her head again.*) That wasn't racist, was it? I'm sorry. I swear. My ex is Latino.

I'm sorry. I talk too much. I say too much dumb stuff. And I forced that toothbrush on you. I'm working on it, but it's…The deodorant aisle is that way. Two aisles down.

American Midget
Jonathan Yukich

> Play
> Female
> 50s
> Comic

Professor Dripworth melodramatically addresses her students on the first day of art class.

PROFESSOR DRIPWORTH:

Let me begin by saying, with abject certitude, that the world will, in time, be destroyed. Of this I'm certain. By bomb, by plague, one day we will cease. So what good is painting? What good is art? When we perish, as we surely will, who will hang the Rembrandts, read the Shakespeares? I'll tell you who: *the aliens.* Look away! Heads down! (…)
(Pauses. Allows for heads going down. Collects herself.)

Yes, pupils, there will be aliens. Of this I'm certain. And, like us, they'll only preserve art suitable to their sensibilities. So we must ask, is our work suitable for aliens? Have we—*you*— anything to offer our successors? This is, as artists, our endgame: to possess talent capable of rallying alien favor. Well, do you have such talent? This is what you're here to find out. Right now. This instant. You will draw, for the appeasement of future colonizing life forms, what is before you. At stake: the glory of humankind.
(She disrobes, wearing only bra and underwear.)

You may lift your heads, pupils.
(She allows them a moment.)

Look upon it, soak it in. I'm no longer your teacher, but your muse. I'm bestowing to you the privilege of fixing a moment in time. The way Picasso fixed Guernica or Monet fixed the light on his lilies, moments to be captured for eons, never to be lost. So now, pupils, make me immortal. Take up your pencils, brave your souls, and etch my figure for the alien ages ahead. Fix me!
(She strikes a pose.)

As You Like It
William Shakespeare

> Play
> Female
> 20+
> Comic

Phoebe wrestles with her affection for Ganymede, unaware that "he" is actually Rosalind in disguise.

PHOEBE:
Think not I love him, though I ask for him.
'Tis but a peevish boy; yet he talks well;
But what care I for words? yet words do well,
When he that speaks them pleases those that hear. It is a pretty
youth: not very pretty:But, sure, he's proud; and yet his pride
becomes him:
He'll make a proper man: the best thing in him
Is his complexion; and faster than his tongue
Did make offence his eye did heal it up.
He is not very tall; yet for his years he's tall:
His leg is but so so; and yet 'tis well:
There was a pretty redness in his lip,
A little riper and more lusty red
Than that mix'd in his cheek; 'twas just the difference
Betwixt the constant red and mingled damask.
There be some women, Silvius, had they mark'd him
In parcels as I did, would have gone near
To fall in love with him; but, for my part,
I love him not nor hate him not; and yet
Have more cause to hate him than to love him:
For what had he to do to chide at me?
He said mine eyes were black and my hair black;
And, now I am remember'd, scorn'd at me.
I marvel why I answer'd not again:
But that's all one; omittance is no quittance.
I'll write to him a very taunting letter,
And thou shalt bear it: wilt thou, Silvius?

Bangs

Irene Ziegler

> Freestanding monologue
> Female
> 50+
> Comic

Your bangs can never be too long, or your miniskirt too short. The opposite is not true.

WOMAN:

When my sisters and I were kids, long bangs were the rage. Beatlemania, dontchaknow. But when hair got in eyes, my mother lost her patience and came at us with the scissors. Not pretty. She always, ALWAYS cut our bangs too short. If you've been on the receiving end of a too-short bang cut, you're feelin' me. The humiliation!

My family calls them Charlie Chocks bangs. Maybe your family calls them Buster Brown bangs. Or perhaps just ugly ass bangs. All are good.

Perhaps this same inclination explains my mother's seeming inability to hem pants without turning them into clam diggers. She still does it! You can say it until you're blue in the face: "Not too short! Not too short!"

Save your breath. You're going to get too short.

On only one occasion did her scissor-happy proclivity come in handy. It was in 1971, and I was sixteen; go-go boots kicked, and miniskirts were the rage. My groovy Aunt June from San Francisco, who shopped at I. Magnin's, sent me white, vinyl go-go boots and the cutest yellow dress of cotton jersey. But the dress hit at the knees and might as well have been a granny gown, as far as I was concerned. There was no way I could wear it to the Homecoming game. I was devastated.

Mom to the rescue. She measured, cut and hemmed three times before she got the hem even all the way around, and my frowsy yellow dress became, to my father's horror, a micro-mini. I couldn't have been happier. Of course, I couldn't bend over, sit down, or raise my arms, but who cared?

Unfortunately, I had the bad sense to let her trim my bangs at the same time. Afterward, Charlie Chocks. But I needn't have worried. As my father was quick to point out, in my new go-go boots and micro-minidress from I. Magnin's, no one was looking at my bangs.

Bereavement Group
Bara Swain

Play
Female
20s-30s
Comic

Michelle, a Korean-American woman, is in a therapist's office with two other patients, waiting for their group therapy session to begin.

MICHELLE:

Okay! Okay! I'll tell you what I lost. It was my sense of purpose, all right? I LOST MY SENSE OF PURPOSE!
(Silence.)

It's been so hard, SO hard, you know? When I was in high school, I knew what I wanted to be. At least, I knew what my father wanted me to be. He wanted me to be a lawyer like Jane Kim. Jane Kim—the first Korean American elected official in San Francisco. Her parents immigrated from Seoul, like my mom and dad. Only I wasn't like Jane Kim. I went to Connecticut College, not Stanford. And I couldn't get into law school. I tried…believe me, I tried! So when Jane Kim ran for the San Francisco Board of Education, I started sewing. My mother thought I could be the next Christina Kim.
(Explaining.)

Dosa. She's the founder of the design house Dosa. Oh, come on, guys. Christina Kim is only the most respected South Korean-born fashion designer in the world! Only I failed at that, too, and, oh, I needed a sense of purpose. And I thought I found one again—I really did—when Beverly Kim won the first "Last Chance Kitchen" on Top Chef.
(Excitedly.)

In Episode 10 she made seared black drum with oranges, fennel and black olives. And I baked my first Swanson Chicken frozen dinner. Then she made grilled lamb chop with parsnips with curry, radicchio and white anchovy vinaigrette on Episode 11. I made a tossed green salad—that was tossed! On Episode 12, Beverly Kim went head to head with Grayson Schmitz and returned to the main competition by her winning red snapper in coconut broth infused with lemongrass, ginger, Thai basil and cilantro.
(Wailing.)

I DON'T EVEN KNOW WHAT CILANTRO IS!

The Big Day

Katy Wix

Freestanding monologue
Female
20s
Comic

Every bride's nightmare: the inappropriate wedding toast, served up British-style.

MAID OF HONOR:

Thank you. Thank you. Thanks so much.

Um, not very good at public speaking and unfortunately I'm not just saying that, so I'll keep it brief. And I'm sure you'll agree with me when I say that the bride looks absolutely ravenous today, absolutely gorgeous—love the hair—really jazzy! And, she was so worried about—because it's very thin isn't it and in bright sunlight—it can go quite see-through can't it, so I'm just glad that the beautiful hair piece arrived on time (…)

So what makes a good wedding speech? Well, I honestly didn't have a clue and I've only been to one wedding myself—last year in Cyprus (and it was awful). So, I decided to Google it and according to the internet, a good speech should "share some funny or touching memories about the bride, honour the bride and groom's relationship and offer up advice and well-wishes as the pair begin their lives together."

Well, that's quite difficult to write, so I haven't done that, but what I have done is to write a list of all the stories that are too inappropriate to talk about, so—you won't be hearing the following:

- you won't hear about the time we snorted coke and went flat-hunting.
- you won't hear about the time we hid someone's EpiPen, as a joke.
- you won't hear about the time we got off with each other in return for free drinks.

None of that stuff.

And your new husband is sat there—look at him—grinning

away like the cat that got the cream, and rightly so. As you know—I didn't like him at first, but now—I get it. Having spent a bit more time with him, I get it now...kinda. It certainly proves that love is blind, I mean, well, no—I just mean it's about making choices that make you happy isn't it, not anyone else, which is great.

And the bride's mother looks stunning today as well. It's actually really sexist that the way wedding speeches always go on about how the women in the room look. It sort of undermines the compliment anyway, doesn't it—when you feel obliged to pay one. Anyway, sorry—the bride's mother really does look lovely. (…) My own mother smoked all throughout my birth—I'm kidding of course! Just trying to get the funnies in...

The Big Hat
Martha Patterson

Play
Female
20s-30s
Comic

In a Kansas City bar, Marnie holds a shot glass of whisky and speaks to the audience.

MARNIE:

(In a Southern accent.) Let me tell you frankly. I'm a slut. And a boozer. And a real dish. And believe me, I let people know. They don't seem to be shocked by my revelations. They just call me "interesting." I draw men to me like flies to molasses. It was partly the influence of my Aunt Alice, you see. She was beautiful. She had dark, billowing hair which she wore loose or piled up in a French twist. And she wore <u>lots</u> of makeup. She also wore perfume. And her clothes! Low-cut, a little too tight, and shoes with the toes cut out. And she smoked Lucky Strikes. So you can obviously see why, at the age of six, I decided I wanted to be just like her. *(Pause.)*

I make an impression when I walk into a room. I was standing on the corner one day when a man hollered at me from across the street. He was probably a lawyer, probably wore a Rolex watch, he was probably drunk, but anyway he yelled, "Honey, you're so sweet you're giving me a toothache." Probably a very old line, but it did make me laugh. *(Pause.)*

Only thing is, I know it's not going to last forever. One of these days I'll start showing my age and, one by one, the men will stop coming. *(Pause.)*

So I have a plan. When I turn 50, I'm going to start wearing hats. *Big hats.* That's what my Aunt Alice would have done. But she disappeared from our lives when she was only 45. She was said to be dyin' of some unknown disease no one knew the cure for. Oh, well. We all gotta go sometime.

Bite Me
Nina Mansfield

> Play
> Female
> 25-35
> Comic

Ellen managed to subdue a vampire with pepper spray, then bring him home in a cage. She tells her baffled husband how she pulled it off.

ELLEN:

So there he is, stunned from the spray. Writhing on the ground like a baby. When WHAM! Got him in the balls. BAM, I hit him with my handbag, and ZANG, got him again with the pepper spray. At that point it was like pure adrenaline! I was on fire! Once I had him subdued I realized the emblem on my Tory Burch handbag is totally cross-like, so I held it up to his face, and sure enough he was like, "Ahh," and I was like, "Take that you creature of the dark," and he was like, "Ahhh," and I was like, "That's what you get for attacking women in alleys," and he's like, "Please, I can't help it! It's just my nature," and I'm like, "I don't care if it's just your nature you woman-hater," and he's like, "Please, I don't hate women, I just want to suck your blood," and I'm like "Ew," and he's like, "You get used to it," and I'm like "really?" and he's like, "Really," and then he started to lunge for me again, 'cause I'd sort of forgotten to hold up my handbag, but I was like really caffein-ated, so my reflexes were on point, so I was like, "Take this!" and he was like, "Ahhh." And then I had this idea. I thought, why not take lemons and turn them into lemonade. I was like, "You scumbag vampire," and he was like, "I'm really not a scumbag," and I was like, "Oh yeah?" and he was like, "Yeah," and so I sprayed him with more pepper spray, and made him drape my handbag over his shoulder, which made him lose like all his powers, and then I loaded him into the back of the Escalade and Voilá!

The Bray of the Belles (#1)

David-Matthew Barnes

> Play
> Female
> Early 30s
> Comic

Madeline, a Southern woman, is at a wedding shower. Fed up with the bragging and boasting that has occurred at the table, she feigns sweetness when talking to Natasha, a despised childhood nemesis. Slowly, Madeline's kind façade crumbles.

MADELINE:

Look at you. So thin and fit. You've got a great figure. And your hair—well, if we didn't know any better, sugar, we would truly believe that icy blonde was a real color. And that little sports car I always see you zooming around town in. Well, I think you look just divine in it. Very glamorous and sexy. Sort of like one of those women who tempt a minister into a life of debauchery and sin. Lord, who knew you'd turn out to be so clever with money? Maybe that's why I feel so much joy for you deep down in my heart, Natasha. Since you came from nothing and your daddy lost the family farm and your mama went to jail for fraud for embezzling money from that church fund raiser we had for the crippled children in Monaco, it makes it all the more special that you've mastered the art of finances. You're a real pro now. I bet you could get a dollar from every man you meet just for being you. It's a good thing Edgar finally put a ring on your finger. To tell you the truth, I was a little nervous you might have ended up in one of those tawdry hot spots in New Orleans trying to secretly care for an illegitimate bastard baby, or ridding your once tarnished soul of a filthy disease you contracted from one of those sailor men you used to be so fond of. But you are living proof that all things get better with time. Wow. You bought *another* house. That's just the best news I've heard all summer. *(Beat.)* Somebody pass me the corn bread. I am famished.

The Bray of the Belles (#2)

David-Matthew Barnes

> Play
> Female
> Early 30s
> Comic

Madeline, a Southern woman, is at a wedding shower. Fed up with the bragging and boasting that has occurred at the table, she feigns sweetness when talking to Natasha, a despised childhood nemesis. Slowly, Madeline's kind façade crumbles.

MADELINE:

Well, that is just the best news I think I have heard in all my life! I'm really, really happy for you. I'm ecstatic. I think my face just might catch fire from the joy I feel. Imagine that! You and Edgar have bought *another* house. How many does that make now? I don't have enough fingers and toes to keep count and like you said us country girls are too simple to know our last names. Nine? Ten? Four hundred and eleven? Mercy, me. You really did grow up and buy the town. The next thing we know you'll be running for Mayor. But don't worry. If you do, I swear on a nameless grave that I will keep my mouth shut about that incident with the Mexican boy who used to work on your daddy's farm. You're just becoming a regular queen of real estate, aren't you? Taking those houses from those poor people who lost their jobs and can't afford their mortgage no more. Then selling it to land developers for a mighty high price. I think you're a genius with a gift from God. I don't know how you sleep at night with the loud rustling of those angels wings that fly around your head. I'm sure you must know that the rest of us are a tad bit jealous of you. Oh, don't look so surprised. It's no secret that you've always gotten everything that you wanted. But you deserve it, honey. Yes, you do. You deserve exactly what you get in this lifetime and the ones to follow.

Brogue
Duncan Pflaster

Freestanding monologue
Female
26-40
Comic

A businesswoman enters and speaks in a passionate rush to her coworker.

WOMAN:

Hi. I'm sorry to have to do this to you, I know you just started here a week ago, but I can't work with you. I can't go on working with you. No, don't say anything. PLEASE don't say anything. I know Jeff assigned us to work on this project, and you're certainly qualified, and you have excellent references...No, please don't speak. Again, let me finish. It's just that...well, you have a Scottish accent. And that just melts me. And you're very beautiful on top of that. No, please don't say anything; my knees begin to buckle every time you speak and my gut churns and I—(...) it's embarrassing. I'm a businesswoman, and it's very important to me to be professional about this. (...) It's just I've always *always* had a thing for brogues. I've considered in the past that perhaps I myself should go to Scotland or Ireland, since there I would be conversely adorably continental, but then on the other hand, I would surely run into the same problem I'm running into here with you, which—were I to be surrounded by brogues, I would—I don't know *what* I'd do. Now, I understand not all women may feel this way about you, or indeed about brogues, so this may seem novel, however I would like to pause for a moment to talk about your hair and what that also does to me. It just glistens in the morning in the sunlight and—well, you see my problem. No, DON'T say anything. If you talk to me, you will be charming and sexy and I may lose my resolve. Thank you. Now. Considering my admiration for you, we have a few choices. We may correspond entirely by e-mail and never see or hear each other. This may seem inconvenient, but no less inconvenient, I assure you, than my constant contemplation of your mellifluous voice. Our other option is for one of us to leave this company. Now, I completely understand you're here in America under a work visa, which requires you to, you know, "work", so I think it best that I be the one to leave the company. I am not ordinarily one to sacrifice, but here I feel it is warranted. So I have given my two-minute notice to Jeff just before I came in here. And now *(looks at watch)* I am no longer employed by the company, so there should be no problems with Human Resources when I ask you if you want to get a drink with me later. *(Beat.)* You can talk now.

By Faith Alone
Marjorie Benton Cooke

> Play
> Female
> 40+
> Comic

It's the early 1900s, and Mrs. Frederick Belmont-Towers has found a marvelous new key to enlightenment.

MRS. TOWERS:

Is that you, Helen? Come in. You must excuse me for seeing you up here, but this is my day for treatment and I don't get up till afternoon. Oh, didn't you know? I'm taking a course with Omarkanandi, this famous Hindu priest. You haven't heard of him? Oh, my dear, he is too wonderful. You know what an invalid I've been for years? I've had no sympathy in my suffering —(...) but Omarkanandi says my condition has been simply pitiful! He's so sympathetic, Helen. He wears a long red robe, and a turban and the queerest rings, and his eyes are the most soulful things. Well, it's hard to tell you just what he does. He sits beside me, and holds my hands and looks into my eyes and talks to me, in his soft Oriental voice. He says he is the medium of infinite strength and power, and that he transmits it to me. Well, he thinks in time that I can draw on this power myself, without him. He says that I'm so highly strung that the winds of evil play on me. He says my chronic indigestion is simply a wind of evil, and that I must harden myself against it. I told him I didn't care so much about the indigestion itself, but it was ruining my complexion. He said when I got myself into harmony with the Infinite my skin would be like a rose leaf—so you can see for yourself the thing is worthwhile.

Check Please
Jonathan Rand

> Play
> Female
> 20s
> Comic

Author's note: Linda's personality switches should be fast. Each personality should be a different level—her voice and demeanor should be changing dramatically throughout.

LINDA:

Hi.

I've been looking forward to this for a while. (…) Hold on. I forgot to—

(She rummages through her purse…)

(…) I've got this pill I need to take or else I get all weird. I know I brought them. They've gotta be—. You know, whatever. I'll be fine. (…) It won't kill me if I don't take it for one night. I just may be a little out of whack. You probably won't even be able to tell. Whatever. So—anyway. (…) it's nice to finally meet you.

(Suddenly sarcastic, morose, in a monotone voice:) Oh yes. It's so awesome to finally put a name with a face.

(Giggly/bubbly:) You're funny; you're cute.

(Gruff:) he's not cute. You just haven't been out in a while.

(Snobby:) That is NOT—TRUE. He is GOOD—LOOKING.

(Jittery:) Shhhhhhhhh…You're embarrassing yourself…

(Aggressive:) Quit freaking out.

(Easily offended:) What? Why are you jumping all over me?

(Little girl:) She started it!

(Motherly:) Girls, don't fight. What would your father say.

(Fatherly:) Oh, let 'em fight. (…)

(Monkey:) Ooh ooh, ah! ah! ah!

(Snobby:) All right, who brought the monkey?

(Assertive:) Not me.

(Little girl:) Not me.

(Gruff:) Not me.

(Pushover:) I did. I'm so sorry.

(Aggressive:) A monkey? Come on!

(Motherly:) You'd better behave yourself young lady, or you're grounded.

(Fatherly:) Get off her case, woman!

(Monkey:) Ooh ooh AHH AAHHH!

(LINDA finds pills.)

(Cheery:) There they are!

(Gruff:) Yeah, took long enough.

(LINDA swallows the pill.)

(Mostly back to normal, but woozy:) Okay. Okay. It's starting to kick in. (…) In a couple of seconds, I'll settle into a single personality. But don't worry—nine times out of ten it's one of the normal ones.

(LINDA lets out a monkey shriek.)

Curio

Katy Wix

Freestanding monologue
Female
20s-30s
Comic

A delightfully delusional British woman believes she is The Virgin Mary, which can cause problems if you have a job and live in the real world.

WOMAN:

Well, you know, I took so many drugs that I ended up thinking I was Mary, the Virgin Mary. Yeah, I totally believed it. And life as the Virgin Mary was pretty pretty good. It was no different really, it was just that I was the Madonna and child, but without the child. (…)

It wasn't a strong dose or anything but I was feeling, maybe a little more receptive than usual. A face appeared to me that looked very much like the Virgin Mary. That floated around a bit and I was just getting comfortable with that and then she spoke and she says: 'You alright?'

and I says, 'Yeah.'

and then she goes, 'You know—you're just like me?'

and I go 'Yeah?'

And she goes, 'Yeah.'

I just thought it was normal, a natural part of reality. Believed she was real, definitely, because my first thought was—oh great, finally—someone wise to talk to—someone who's lived a bit—been around a while.

It was euphoric actually, at the time.

I went home, still high. Went to sleep, woke up the next morning and I thought, 'Oh yeah—I'm the Virgin Mary.' They were a bit freaked out in the shop because I turned up with a blue scarf draped over my head and like I didn't really reference it all day, so they didn't say anything. I think it would've been fine, you know, because it's quite a trendy part of town and I think they just would have thought—oh well, it's probably a new fashion thing or whatever. I made it worse though 'cos, and I don't totally remember this, but I asked my boss for the rest of the week off? And she said, Oh why, are you unwell? And I said, no, I've got to give birth to Jesus.

And of course, I was sent home. Which, looking back, was stupid because I needed the money. (…)

Dead and Breathing
Chisa Hutchinson

> Play
> Female
> 30s-40s
> Comic

Veronika, an African-American home-care nurse has seen. Some. Things.

VERONIKA:

Yes ma'am, I saw a lot of weird stuff in the ER, but that tops 'em all. In fact, that's right about when I decided to get into caring for the elderly. Shit. Old people are generally wise enough to know a watermelon's got no place up their ass. You gotta appreciate the man's sense of adventure, though. I bet he's a real hoot in bed. Or in the produce aisle—ha! If he worked at a grocery store and got an employee discount, that'd be like an endless sale on sex toys for him. That'd be some shit, wouldn't it? You think his coworkers ever suspected him of being food fetishist? Can you imagine? "Mr. Smith, is that a cucumber in your pocket or are you just happy to see me?" HA! That wasn't his name, by the way—Mr. Smith. I changed the name to protect the... well I was gonna say the innocent, but I think a watermelon up the ass pretty much precludes you from that category. Hell, the watermelon may've been the only innocent party up in that camp. Still. I wouldn't put the man's business out on the street like that. It's illegal. And unprofessional. And I am nothing if not professional.

The Dutch Courtesan

John Marston

> Play
> Female
> 20s
> Comic

Crispinella allows her friend's husband as an exception to the otherwise tainted pool of married men. Or does she?

CRISPINELLA:

Marry? No, faith; husbands are like lots in the lottery: you may draw forty blanks before you find one that any prize in him. A husband generally is a careless, domineering thing that grows like coral, which as long as it is under water is soft and tender, but as soon as it has got his branch above the waves is presently hard, stiff, not to be bowed but burst; so when your husband is a suitor and under your choice, Lord, how supple his is, how obsequious, how at your service, sweet lady! Once married, got up his head above, a stiff, crooked, knobby, inflexible, tyrannous creature he grows; then they turn like water: more you would embrace, the less you hold. I'll live my own woman, and if the worst come to the worst, I had rather price a wag than a fool. (…)

But thy match, sister, by my troth, I think 'twill do well. He's a well-shaped, clean-lipped gentleman, of a handsome but not affected fineness, a good faithful eye, and a well-humored cheek.

Eve's Diary
Mark Twain

> Play
> Female
> 20s
> Comic

The first woman in biblical creation notates her first days with the odd being, Adam.

EVE:

We are getting along very well now, Adam and I, and getting better and better acquainted. He does not try to avoid me anymore, which is a good sign, and shows that he likes to have me with him. That pleases me, and I study to be useful to him in every way I can, so as to increase his regard. During the last day or two I have taken all the work of naming things off his hands, and this has been a great relief to him, for he has no gift in that line, and is evidently very grateful. He can't think of a rational name to save him, but I do not let him see that I am aware of his defect. Whenever a new creature comes along I name it before he has time to expose himself by an awkward silence. In this way I have saved him many embarrassments. I have no defect like this. The minute I set eyes on an animal I know what it is. I don't have to reflect a moment; the right name comes out instantly, just as if it were an inspiration, as no doubt it is, for I am sure it wasn't in me half a minute before. I seem to know just by the shape of the creature and the way it acts what animal it is. When the dodo came along he thought it was a wildcat—I saw it in his eye. But I saved him. And I was careful not to do it in a way that could hurt his pride. I just spoke up in a quite natural way of pleasing surprise, and not as if I was dreaming of conveying information, and said, "Well, I do declare, if there isn't the dodo!" I explained—without seeming to be explaining—how I know it for a dodo, and although I thought maybe he was a little piqued that I knew the creature when he didn't, it was quite evident that he admired me. That was very agreeable, and I thought of it more than once with gratification before I slept. How little a thing can make us happy when we feel that we have earned it!

Exit, Pursued by a Bear (#3)

Lauren Gunderson

> Play
> Female
> 19-21
> Comic

Sweetheart, a North Georgian, is an ex-stripper-turned-actor who is assisting Nan with a plot to end Nan's abusive husband's life. It's the best role she's ever had.

SWEETHEART:

Two months ago I was on my way to audition for *Hamlet* at the Dahlonega Community Players when I first saw Nan. She was at the Subway just tearing through this foot long with all that stringy lettuce and crying and mauling those poor SunChips.

And I thought – this is real drama. Investigate.

So I asked her if she needed anything. And she told me that she didn't believe in love or justice anymore.

And I was like: whoa. Deep drama, y'all.

So I told her I was going to this audition—cause *Hamlet's* got some major justice, kids. And she went with me, and then we got some food at the Chick-fil-A, and it was over those super puffy waffle fries that we became friends. I told her about my dreams of acting (I did not get the role of Hamlet, however), and she told me about her dream of saving animals (she works at this small vet in Canton), and I gave her my copy of *The Collected works of William Shakespeare*, and she gave me free cat checkups.

I even told her I was stripping at the Highway Club until I got my big break. And she didn't hate me for it. Which some people do.

And after a month of sharing books and meals and funny LOL cat pictures—she told me about Kyle and love and justice and how there was a bigger truth at stake if only she had the courage. And I said…

Let's get classical.

Experience
Katy Wix

> Freestanding monologue
> Female
> Unspecified Age
> Comic

A British woman believes she was abducted by aliens and, consequently, knows some heavy shit.

WOMAN:

Well, you're in for a wonderful treat ... because *I am* going to tell *you* the truth. Uh oh! What did she just say!? Yeah, the truth. Sounds scary? Well, it is...n't.

'Truth', defined in the dictionary as 'a proven or verified...,' I don't know, I'm making it up, but it's impressive isn't it when people do that—when people throw in a dictionary definition, like when I was in the debating society at school and we employed the same technique, thus winning the argument and, finally, proving that racism was wrong. I think I've misremembered that. (...)

Sorry, this is difficult for me.

The truth is, I'm a liar. Or to put it another way; the truth was a lie and I'm not lying. The hypnotherapy wasn't for fear of flying. I actually love flying. I love the fact you can't be contacted. No, my reason for having it was for more...alien abductionry ... related...reasons.

Padma (that's my hypnotherapist) told me to be careful about whom I reveal my secret to. I just believe, and have done for some time, that I was probed...well maybe not probed, but tampered with certainly, by hybrid...other beings...I don't have a name for them ... sods, haha.

(Pointing upwards.)

That mob!

Yeah. This is serious shit.

And you know how, like, I always come across as a really fearful person—so I jump when the toast pops and I Google sinkholes? Well, this is why. Something happened to me. And now, thanks to my sessions with Padma, I have gone from total despair to just mild depression, which I think is a huge step forward. (...)

The Far-Flung
Julie McKee

Play
Female
60s
Comedy

Mrs. Gilbert, a parishioner at St. Luke's Anglican Church in the provincial town of Papakura, New Zealand, would very much like to have a larger (or, at least, more exotic) part in the upcoming pageant, organized in honor of Queen Victoria, who is to visit.

MRS. GILBERT:

Are we to have a rehearsal, do you think? (…)

I do love the theatre, don't you? I always wanted to play Camille. I see myself as a tragedienne, you see. Wouldn't think it to look at me though, would you? No, I suppose not. I always wanted to be St. Joan, you know that sort of a part. Heroic, going up in flames. But I had to give it up when I got married. My husband, you see.

In the dark recesses of his limited mind, I know there must be a fondness for the theatre, but I've never been able to drag it out of him. He's an atheist by nature. A gardener, growing vegetables which is why he doesn't bother much with religion. Says it's all there in your vegetable. Take your tomato, for instance. You plant the seed, you water it, it grows, you eat it, you…and so on and so forth. Nature, you see. Very fond of nature. He wants to be buried in our backyard, underneath the tomatoes, but trouble is, after I'm gone, some bugger's going to come along and buy the house, and what happens then, ay? He doesn't believe in graveyards. He reckons I'd never come to visit him in one of them, because they're so far away and he's right, I wouldn't. How would I get there, ay? Ever think of that?

Fourteen
Alice Gerstenberg

> Play
> Female
> 40s
> Comic

Mrs. Pringle, a woman of fashion, is preparing to host a dinner party to introduce her daughter and it must be perfect. Perfect, do you hear? Perfect!

MRS. PRINGLE:

I shall go mad! I'll never entertain again—never—never—people ought to know whether they're coming or not—but they accept and regret and regret and accept—they drive me wild. This is my last dinner party—my very last—a fiasco—an utter fiasco! A haphazard crowd—hurried together—when I had planned everything so beautifully—now how shall I seat them—how shall I seat them? If I put Mr. Tupper here and Mrs. Conley there, then Mrs. Tupper has to sit next to her husband and if I want Mr. Morgan there—Oh! It's impossible—I might as well put their names in a hat and draw them out at random—never again! I'm through! Through with society—with parties—with friends—I wipe my slate clean—they'll miss my entertainments—they'll wish they had been more considerate—after this, I'm going to live for myself! I'm going to be selfish and hard—and unsociable—and drink my liquor myself instead of offering it gratis to the whole town!—I'm through—Through with men like Oliver Farnsworth!—I don't care how rich they are! How influential they are—how important they are! They're nothing without courtesy and consideration—business—off on train—nonsense—didn't want to come—didn't want to meet a sweet, pretty girl—didn't want to marry her—well, he's not good enough for you!—don't you marry him! Don't you dare marry him! I won't let you marry him! Do you hear? If you tried to elope or anything like that, I'd break it off—yes, I would—Oliver Farnsworth will never get recognition from me!—He is beneath my notice! I hate Oliver Farnsworth!

Friday Night is For Relaxing, Right? Sure it is.

Suzan Hyssen

> Blog
> Female
> 25+
> Comic

It began so simply, so innocently. And THEN...

WOMAN:

How was your Friday night?

Mine was terrible, thanks.

I got stung by a wasp that was IN MY HAIR.

I fucking hate nature.

Yeah, so I thought I'd be a grown up and go to the market to get some fresh fruits and veggies to make for dinner. Instead, I end up getting stung, having a panic attack, going to urgent care, and also involving my neighbor.

The husband was at work, and was going to be late. I drove home from the market, and, for who knows what reason, I reached into my purse for something. I felt a pretty painful jab, but figured it was the teeth on the zipper of my bag snagging my forearm. What else could it possibly be, right?

My right arm and hand started feeling funny and weird—buzzy and tense and ache-y—but I thought it was maybe because I pack-mule carried too many bags to my car. I kept flexing my arm and fingers and looked for a cut or something, but I didn't see anything. Also, I was driving, so I wasn't looking too close.

I pulled into the garage and turned off the car and, because I am vain and always want to look at myself, checked the rearview mirror. And there is a wasp. IN. MY. HAIR.

I screamed.

And realized I didn't get snagged by my zipper, I got stung.

And then I really started panicking, because I had been stung by a wasp, and it was in my hair, and I was alone having to deal with this.

I debated just laying down and dying, but my manicure was pretty terrible, and also there were a lot of groceries in the car and I didn't want to waste that money.

(...) So I took my keys and opened the car door, and nudged the wasp onto my keys, which I immediately shook outside the car and then slammed the door shut.

And continued to panic.

(…) I went next door, and my nice neighbor drove me to the urgent care. Probably the most comical part was getting in and out of his very giant truck. I am not tall. It was like practicing the high jump.

Then at the urgent care, they put me in the pediatrics room. I'd like to think that it was because it was the only room available, but it was probably because I was a big fucking baby.

I managed to calm down, finally, and because I tend to end up with double size reactions to bee stings, I got some steroids for the sting. The after-effects of the panic attack and a nice dose of Benadryl, and I was asleep by 9pm.

Next Friday night? Taco Goddamn Bell for dinner.

Ghost of a Chance

Pamela Hooks

> Freestanding monologue
> Female
> 35+
> Comic

Toni, a real estate agent, shows a young couple a house she knows is haunted.

TONI:

And this ...um... is the living room. Aptly called, don't you think? I mean...what else would one do here...except...live, right? Certainly not...not live.

Excuse me, I have to light some sage. It's okay. It helps get rid of, not smells, but you know. Other things.

Oh, no: I do this whenever I show clients a home. I believe you are entitled to a clean slate, a fresh view ... devoid of the...past...

(Looking around warily.)

With no trace—no trace you hear me?—Of the former... inhabitants. Out with the old!

(Under her breath:)

From Hell you come, to Hell you are going
through the monastery of the Creator
where good people are lifted up
and the evil are pushed down...
WHAT THE HELL IS THAT?!
Oh, nothing. Sorry. ANYway...

The owner has gone waaaaaay down on the price. Actually, it looks a lot better in here than I thought it would. Modern forensics has come a long way. You can get blood out of grout, now, apparently. Hey, technology. I'm all for it.

Half-bath over there in the corner. I don't care to open the door, but you go right ahead.

And through there is the kitchen. Note the well-seasoned butcher-block countertop and convenient meat hooks hanging above.

If you see a bowling ball bag, don't open it. Ha ha...it's a ... joke...

Listen, I'm going to let you kids look around. I'll be in my car. If...it's still there.

Goodbye Charles (#1)

Gabriel Davis

Play
Female
17-25
Comic

Cynthia shuts down a proposal.

CYNTHIA:

Don't do it! Don't open that little box one more crack! Don't ask me to marry you. Shh, shh, shh. Don't say another word. Just listen.

I can't let you do this to me. I mean, before I met you I used be such a jerk. I mean, seriously, everyone at work thought I was a huge jerk. No one actually liked me. Those people I introduced to you as my friends. They're not my friends. They're scared of me.

But since being with you, I've begun to feel all...warm inside. Fuzzy. I find myself wanting to stroll in the park and whistle!

I have these thoughts, these urges to donate to charities and help out in soup kitchens, and hug people.

Don't you see? Don't you see you're making me NICE!? And what really scares me is that you'll open that box and ask me to marry you, and I'll...I'll just nicely say "yes," and then I'll be nice for life.

Please, for the love of God, put that box away. I mean, the planet already has millions of nice people. It doesn't need me too. Please, stop, don't—I'm asking you—no, I'm begging you—I'm getting down on my knees.

Will you please, please not marry me?

The Gulf (#1)
Audrey Cefaly

Play
Female
20s-40s
Comic

Betty, from Alabama, has opinions.

BETTY:

Did you know that Dolores Pettaway has 15 cats? I mean I knew she had a lot of cats but that is a *lotta* fuckin cats. And she's not like fostering them or whatever. She's just *collecting* them. Like stamps. Until they die, or she dies, or somebody calls the cops. It's so bad over there, Lord, it's infested with fleas and it stinks so bad, I was jumpin' outta my socks. I bet not one of them 15 cats is spayed or neutered, what do you think? She's on welfare, she's got the EBT, I found that out. Deanna told me she comes in to the Winn Dixie twice a week and that's all she buys is cat food. Tons and tons of Meow Mix and Friskies. Oh, and the National Enquirer. She gets that on Mondays. I think I must have been having a cat dream and woke up to talkin' about cats or somethin'. I just don't know how you feed all those cats if you're on welfare. Wait. You don't think she eats cat food, do you? Well now I wanna check the price of cat food. Why am I talking about this? Oh, yeah. I remember. Everybody at the bar is taking turns feeding the cats for Miss Dolores while she's up in Foley at her mama's funeral. I told 'em I didn't want to go over there by myself. It's too creepy. What if maybe all them cats are like therapeutic or whatever...ya know, like a service dog? Well, why else would you need 15 cats? If the average person is fine with say 1 to 3 cats...and she needs 15 of 'em, then who's to say she's wrong and they're right, I mean, there's not like a rule or anything. Like a *rule of cats*.

The Gulf (#2)
Audrey Cefaly

> Play
> Female
> 20s-40s
> Comic

Betty, from Alabama, spins a mean yarn. And you better listen up, Kendra.

BETTY:

It's warm, idn't it? I might hop in for a swim if I didn't think the gators would get me. No tellin' what's in there. You can't be too careful, you hear about that woman on the news from over in St. Bernard Parish, she gave her baby a bath one night and two days later he died from one of them brain-eatin' amoebas. Brain-eatin' amoebas! I'm just tellin' you, I don't trust it. Where was I? Oh, right. So, theoretically, you could be just as happy as a garbage collector. They have the least amount of stress as any job, you know that? I read that someplace. And think about it. What do they have to be stressed about anyway, except maybe, you know, some maggots and dead rats and whatnot? And you know what...I bet after a couple weeks even the maggots would just be routine, whaddya reckon? Hello? You know what, you need to take a good hard look at yourself, Kendra. You sit there and you pretend not to listen and take full advantage of my stories in all their vivid detail and then you turn on me like a damn dog and give me shit for tellin' em in the first place, and you can't have it both ways, Kendra, you just can't. Where is the respect for the story-teller?? I am fucking delightful!

Her Tongue (#1)

Henry Arthur Jones

> Play
> Female
> 20s-30s
> Comic

In this scene from the 1915 British play, Miss Patty Hanslope is expecting Mr. Walter Scobell to propose. She learns he has nothing of the sort in mind. He apologies for having caused her any… inconvenience.

PATTY:

Inconvenience! I haven't had any breakfast! And I had a most pressing invitation to the Barringers'. They're quite the nicest people in Southsea—one meets everybody there. Instead of that you bring me over here on the distinct understanding that you intended—I don't understand your conduct, Mr. Scobell. Will you please give me some explanation of it? (…) Surely, Mr. Scobell, you will not dare to leave me in this terrible uncertainty. Before you go on board we must please have a thorough understanding. Will you or will you not please give me some explanation of your conduct? (…) Not that I wish to force myself upon you! Please don't think that. I could never stoop to make myself cheap to any man! I'm not driven to that necessity! No! No! A thousand times no! It's simply that my womanly pride and delicacy have been cruelly outraged. It's simply that I owe it to my sense of what is due to an English lady not to be dragged over from Southsea without any breakfast, and then made the sport of your caprice, while you sail off to Argentina, utterly oblivious of your honour, and of the woman you have entangled and deserted! (…)

There will come a time when you will vainly remember how recklessly you threw away the happiness that is still with your grasp, if you only choose to pick it up. *(Suddenly bursting out.)* Oh! What have I said? What have I said? Oh! *(With a long wail she bursts into tears, flings herself over the table and sobs.)*

Her Tongue (#2)
Henry Arthur Jones

> Play
> Female
> 20s-30s
> Comic

In this 1915 British play, Miss Patty Hanslope's cousin, Minnie Brace, and her husband Fred have been advising Patty on how best to win a proposal from Mr. Scobell. Patty has her own plans—especially when she hears that Mr. Scobell is a "very cold, quiet, reserved man."

PATTY:

Then he'll naturally want somebody who is very gay and lively. (…)

My dear Minnie, that shows how little you know about human nature. People are always attracted by their opposites. I'm very glad you've told me Mr. Scobell is cold and reserved, because now I know exactly how to manage him. I was going to be a little reserved and standoffish myself, but now, well, I shall be a little, just a little (*silly little laugh*) free and easy, so as to fit completely into his moods. Why are you two looking at each other like that? Do let me know how to manage my own love affairs. Really any one would think I'd never had (*silly little laugh*) a proposal before!

High Grass
Irene Ziegler

> Play
> Female
> 30s
> Comic

Marsha and Bruce have volunteered to clean up a stretch of county road. Marsha is new in the area and trying to fit in. Bruce does his best to ignore her.

MARSHA:

Hey.

HEY!

Sorry, hi. I'm Marsha. And you're…?

Bruce. Cool.

So. Pretty nice day, right? I mean, the leaves! So gorgeous this time of year. Nature's palette. You couldn't ask for a better day for Community Clean-Up.

I guess you're an old hand at this roadside trash pick-up thing, huh? My first year. We moved into The Chalets in June. The views, you know? I mean, wow.

Kinda fun, too, right? I mean, picking up the things people throw away, it's like an archeological dig out here. Every look at it that way? Like, we're aliens from the future or something, learning about this 21st century American country culture, digging for clues to see if we can stop the coming Apocalypse. You ever think about stuff like that?

No? Huh.

I have to tell you, I haven't been feeling so great lately, so this is kinda like therapy for me. Current affairs, need I say more? I haven't lit up my mind, or committed an act of kindness, or challenged myself physically for a few days now. That's why I signed up for the Clean-Up. I thought this would be a good way to break out of this whatever-it-is. And after this I thought maybe I'd get involved in local politics. Try to do some good in that way. Maybe run for city council.

Oh! You know what we should do? We should create like a mandala out of the things we find, you know? Like a symbolic microcosm of the universe!

Oh, look! My first object! So exciting. *(Beat.)* Oh, jeez, what IS that? Is it a diaper? Omigod, I can smell it from here. MotherFUCKER!

Honky (#1)
Greg Kalleres

Play
Female
25-35
Comic

Andie sits in bed reading Vogue *as she speaks to her husband, Peter, offstage.*

ANDIE:

Oh, my parents called! They want to know what we're doing for the holiday weekend. I said I'd ask you but I think they want us to go up to Connecticut. They're gonna have the Brennans up. Remember the Brennans? Mr. Brennan's the one who smells like mayonnaise. Apparently, they're family now! For the past few months my parents keep referring to them as Aunt and Uncle for some reason. Oh, that reminds me, I haven't told you this yet because my therapist and I are still kind of working it out but I'm pretty sure I have a repressed memory of Mr. Brennan touching me as a kid.

I mean, it's repressed, so you never know for sure but I get a queasy, after school special type of feeling around him. And whenever he sees me in a bathing suit he gives me this very specific sort of: "Whoa, I think I may have molested you once" kind of look. Plus when I go to sleep in my old house, I have this immediate craving for a turkey sandwich. You know. Turkey? Mayo? Probably means nothing but my therapist is gonna think about it. So, anyway, Mom asked the other day if we wanted Mr. Brennan to do our wedding service because he's some sort of judge and I was like, "are you kidding?" Can you see us up there saying our vows and I suddenly smell Miracle Whip and have a panic attack?!

How Water Behaves
Sherry Kramer

> Play
> Female
> 20s
> Comic

Nan lost her purse to a thief at a poetry reading. Allen found and returned it. When he asks where Nan's husband is, she makes up her husband's life, rather than admit he left after a fight.

NAN:

My husband? My husband is at work of course. He works... he works for... a charitable organization. Like the Bill and Melinda Gates Foundation, only smaller. Much smaller. Of course, size isn't everything, it's the work that matters. And my husband's charity does very important work, it well...well...well...it digs wells! His charity drills wells in Africa! It's called All's Well When It Ends With a Well. It was started by theatre people. He makes almost... nothing, that's why losing all our Christmas money is sort of a blow. We have this arrangement, one of us has the money job, and the other one has the repairing the world job. I got stuck with the money job. The problem is, the money job doesn't actually make very much. Money. I wish I had the repair of the world job. When you work at a place like All's Well When It Ends With a Well, or, say, the Bill and Melinda Gates Foundation, you work with very evolved people. You work with people who care about things, and I bet you can take as long a lunch as you like, because your long lunches are with *other* people who are also trying to repair the world, you're working to make the world better during breakfast, lunch, and dinner. Everyone's fair and kind to each other, and everybody's ideas are given equal consideration. And nobody cares about things like fashion or pro-football or anything trivial, nobody in your office has a face lift or gets Botox. All the paper is recycled effortlessly, the coffee in the coffee room is fair trade organic, and it's always the right temperature without ever turning the heat or air conditioning turning on. It's like a temple, a sacred place. Sometimes, I imagine that I am Melinda Gates. I am wearing a white sari with patterns woven with gold threads in it and I am saving the world from malaria.

(A sweeping gesture with her hand.)

I just wave my hand and poof—the mosquitos are vaporized. I go to a leper colony—I hand out state of the art pharmaceuticals Bill has cooked up in his spare time using a logarithm he found stuck on the bottom of his shoe while running a marathon to cure world-wide wall eye. I walk through the streets of Bombay handing out Microsoft Word to infant programmers so they can pull their families out of poverty by the age of three. My hair blows in the breeze. I wear no makeup, but I look refreshed and dewy at all times. I walk through the crowds like a good-looking Mother Theresa.

An Ideal Husband
Oscar Wilde

Play
Female
20s
Comic

In Wilde's classic comedy, Mabel Chiltern bemoans the plight of an oft-proposed-to young woman.

MABEL:

Well, Tommy has proposed to me again. Tommy really does nothing but propose to me. He proposed to me last night in the Music-room, when I was quite unprotected, as there was an elaborate trio going on. I didn't dare to make the smallest repartee, I need hardly tell you. If I had, it would have stopped the music at once. Musical people are so absurdly unreasonable. They always want one to be perfectly dumb at the very moment when one is longing to be absolutely deaf. Then he proposed to me in broad daylight this morning, in front of that dreadful statue of Achilles. Really, the things that go on in front of that work of art are quite appalling. The police should interfere. At luncheon I saw by the glare in his eyes that he was going to propose again, and I just managed to check him in time by assuring him that I was a bimetallist. Fortunately I don't know what bimetallism means. And I don't believe anybody else does either. But the observation crushed Tommy for ten minutes. He looked quite shocked. And then Tommy is so annoying in the way he proposes. If he proposed at the top of his voice, I should not mind so much. That might produce some effect on the public. But he does it in a horrid confidential way. When Tommy wants to be romantic he talks to one just like a doctor. I am very fond of Tommy, but his methods of proposing are quite out of date. I wish, Gertrude, you would speak to him, and tell him that once a week is quite often enough to propose to any one, and that it should always be done in a matter that attracts some attention.

In Which I Counsel Serena Williams About the Girls
Irene Ziegler

Freestanding monologue
Female
25+
Comic

An open letter to Serena Williams after the US Open, 2009.

WOMAN:

Dear Serena (may I?),

What are you, about a 38 triple-F? Was that too personal? Gosh, I'm sorry, but ever since you threatened that lineswoman with severe bodily harm, I've felt a deep personal connection to you. In fact, I wonder if I can have your cell phone number, because there's a woman at the DMV I'd like you to visit on my behalf.

But that's not what I wanted to talk with you about. I wanted to talk to you about, well, your rack.

No, not your racket, your rack. Serena, I must be blunt. In the name of fair competition, I think it's time you hobbled the girls.

Hear me out. At Wimbledon, your fastest serve was clocked at close to 130 mph. No woman has ever hit a tennis ball that hard. And no other woman has had a torpedo deck like yours, either. Coincidence? I think not. Didn't you hear the commentators talking about the "new technology" and how enormous people with tree trunks for legs will set the new standard? If this keeps going, tennis is going to be all about big breasted women serving bullets. If you were to reduce the size of your chest, Serena, you would slow down this ridiculous escalation. Something in a modest B+ or C- would stop the madness.

Talk it over with Venus, your mother, your coach. See if they don't agree that a more streamlined silhouette will help your game. You owe it to the future of the sport.

Excuse me? Your game doesn't need any help? Well, maybe not right now, but...oh, I see. You like yourself just the way you are, and you're not responsible for the future of tennis. Well, it sounds like you've made up your mind then. I'll change the subject. About your badonkadonk...

The Intelligent Design of Jenny Chow: An Instant Message with Excitable Music (#1)

Rolin Jones

> Play
> Female
> 22
> Comic

Jennifer, 22, is Chinese-American, a rapid-fire talker and multi-tasker with OCD, agoraphobia, and fierce computer skills. She talks remotely to a freelance bounty hunter she will hire to find her runaway robot replica. This is of GREAT importance.

JENNIFER:

Okay, so this firewall is serious. Have you installed it yet? *(Pause.)* Yes, go ahead, check. *(A "hacker alert" noise from the computer. To the audience. Pause.)* Oh, that's cute. *(She types in something and the "alert" noise stops. She sprays the computer screen with disinfectant. We hear a "blip" noise from the computer.)* You find missing people, I do the computer stuff. Because next time we're in the middle of an IM and you try to break into my computer, I will send an f-bomb of kiddie porn that will bury itself in your hard drive and spam itself back to every sickfuck pedophile in the world currently under Interpol investigation, okay? I got viruses that can make you piss on yourself and I'm saying this, okay, not because I wouldn't have done the same thing, but because YOU REALLY NEED TO PAY ATTENTION. It's been three days since Jenny got loose. Every second counts. My encryption cannot be broken. Understand? (…) Okay, so here we go….my name is Jennifer Marcus ad I was born in a village outside of Maigon-ko, China, twenty-two years ago and…I'm a girl, duh, and I live in a gated community in Calabasas, California. One of the first things you're going to have to get used to is that I'm better than you. Wait, I'm not being conceited, not really, you know, there's a lot of baggage that comes with it. (…) Oh yeah, and I'm rich. Not super rich. Just regular rich. I feel it's important that you know a little about me, and trust me, okay, you'll need it for the job. This isn't your average runaway case, okay?

The Intelligent Design of Jenny Chow: An Instant Message with Excitable Music (#2)

Rolin Jones

> Play
> Female
> 22
> Comic

Jennifer, 22, is Chinese-American, a rapid-fire talker and multi-tasker with OCD, agoraphobia, and fierce computer skills. She is talking remotely to a freelance bounty hunter she will hire to find her runaway robot replica. This is of GREAT importance. She is typing at a breathtaking speed.

JENNIFER:

Dr. Yakunin says I can trust you. But just because you have a reference like that doesn't mean we're going to work together or that I don't have other options, okay? Let's just say, I've done some research and I know your competition. Ramierez? Bloomstedt? Okay? So I'm not going to take a lot of clandestine bullshit, all right? *(We hear a "blip" noise from the computer)* Good. 'Cause I don't want you to think I'm some sort of bitch, okay? I'm not. I'm a lot of fun. Okay, so this is what I know about you. You were a decorated Army Ranger most assigned to search-and-rescue missions. You've been a freelance bounty hunter ever since you retired and you work alone. (…) You have a near sixty-percent capture rate which I'm told in your line of work is something close to astonishing and which makes me think, you have some serious low expectations for your yourself. Okay soooo, you've never been married but you like prostitutes, although you might want to avoid the young ones in the greater DC area considering the amount of sperm you donated as an undergrad at Georgetown, okay? *(Hits herself in the head.)* Wait, I wasn't supposed to say that. That was my joke to Todd. (Why am I talking about Todd?) I'll tell you about Todd later. That was stupid, cause hey, you know, I've had dreams of sleeping with my dad, who hasn't? But they're never sexy and it's fucking gross, you know? Okay, weird. I'm a weirdo. Soooo we got off track for a sec, and now we're gonna get back on it.

(…) Be right back. (…) I'm really busy, Dad.

Jean's Bean
Ian Richardson

> Play
> Female
> 30s
> Comic

Jean, British, is sitting cross-legged in her living room, contemplating a ceramic plant pot.

JEAN:

Aum. Aum. Aum, bloody aum.

This is my bean. Or rather it will be my bean when it comes up. If it comes up. I saw my friend Carlie's bean yesterday. It's enormous. Which hardly seems fair.

I went and got a lovely ceramic pot, some Peruvian organic compost and a watering thingie from eBay. I'd prepared a lovely little home for it. Carlie put hers in a yoghurt pot.

It was a City Transition idea, "A thousand beans for the City." We'd all raise up a seedling and then all the harvest would go to the foodbank. I'm not sure mine will do much to combat hunger.

I tried singing to it. Thursday night I put it in the middle of the living room and dug out some old Prodigal tracks. I'm not sure 'Twisted Fire Starter' was its cup of tea though. And I may have spilled some wine on it. Maybe the beans will taste of Cab Sauv.

If I get a bean.

I've been leaving talk radio on for it while I'm at work. Which may not have been a good idea. If I listened to the news every day I'm not sure I'd come out either.

Carlie just put hers in a cupboard for a bit and then stuck it on the window sill. Did I mention her bean's enormous? It's like something from the Amazonian rainforest. Troops of Capuchin monkeys could swing through the leaves of hers. This is a nice pot though.

I have a theory. I may have made a bit of a mistake. After the workshop, where they gave us the beans and explained the nutritional gains inherent in a legume based diet, I did a bit of shopping for breakfast the next day. Then, you know, worked my way home, stopping off for a drink, just here and there. And then I got home and planted the bean.

So there is a small possibility that I may have been tending a roasted coffee bean. The next morning the coffee did taste a little odd, but then my mouth tasted a bit funny any way. And my head hurt.

But I have to tell you, I think I may keep it. I've rather enjoyed having someone to care for. It's nice to have the company.

Jeeves Takes a Bow
Margaret Raether

> Play
> Female
> 35-50
> Comic

New York, 1932. Vivienne Duckworth, a bespectacled, serious-minded Englishwoman on her first visit to the States, connives to get tough-guy "Knuckles" McCann to escort her to the underbelly of the city to research her new book, New York, A Modern Gomorrah.

VIVIENNE:

Mr. McCann, I have lived my entire life in strict propriety, cooped up in Much Middleford, Shropshire. And 'til you have been cooped up in Much Middleford, sir, you don't know what cooping is! The only time we get any excitement is when one of the choir-boys is caught sneaking chocolate during the sermon. And let me assure you, Mr. McCann, when that occurs, we talk about it for weeks! Weeks!

(…) Well said. Yowsa, indeed! Today is the first opportunity in my entire life that I have had a real chance to yield to the temptations of a great city. What is the use of a great city having temptations if people do not yield to them? Think how discouraging that must be for a great city! (…) Mr. McCann, how can I possibly write a book that will inspire others to fight with a stout heart against the glamour and fascination of this dreadful city, unless I myself experience that same glamour and fascination first hand? I appeal to you, Mr. McCann, can't you—*won't* you help me to go forth and sin?

Jesus Hates Me (#3)

Wayne Lemon

> Play
> Female
> 43
> Comic

Annie runs a Bible-themed miniature golf course consisting of Wal-Mart mannequins dressed as Bible characters. She is assisted by her son, Ethan, who feels trapped in this small Texas town. Here, Annie defends Jesus against Ethan's post-modern assertions.

ANNIE:

Jesus was not queer. Lots of straight men live with their mothers until they're thirty. You're past twenty, and you still live with me.

And the whole "betrayed with a kiss" thing says way more about Judas than it does our Lord. So what if he didn't have a girlfriend, he had women dripping off him. Mary Magdalene was a whore for crying out loud. Big old sign flashing "hetero hetero." If Jesus was gay, how do you explain her?

She was *not* a fag hag.

I'm going to pray for you. Not now because I don't have time, but later.

Last night's storm. Pretty cool. Thunder, lightning. Wind whipping around like something off the Weather Channel.

Jesus blew off the cross again. Hand me that duct tape. I was hoping the Super Glue'd work. Said on TV it'd hold anything. Apparently they never tested it on the Son of God.

Wise Man blew off his camel over at the first hole, dinged the Christ Child. One of the Ungrateful Lepers lost a foot on eight. The Woman Caught in Adultery ended up facedown in the driveway next door. Harve Oglesby backed over, sheered her head off. Claims he didn't see her but the tire track runs the entire length of her body so I don't know who he thinks he's fooling.

Jesus Hates Me (#5)
Wayne Lemon

> Play
> Female
> 23
> Comic

Lizzy, part-owner of a bar in a small Texas town, confides in Ethan, a restless man she has loved hopelessly since they were kids.

LIZZY:

Christ, Ethan, what happened to us? What are we still doing here?

Lately I find myself going over the events of my life in a meaningless attempt to narrow down the exact day, the exact hour, the exact moment when it all turned to shit.

I'm five years old and my daddy announces it's time we meet Santa Claus live and in the flesh, so he loads me and Georgie in that ancient El Camino and he drives for miles to some godforsaken mall down near the border and the whole way he's playing this *Dean Martin Sings the Sounds of the Season* tape he got free for trying *Readers Digest* for ten days only I don't care because I am finally going to get to whisper directly into Santa's ear exactly what I want for Christmas. No more unanswered letters, no more lying awake Christmas Eve wondering if he'll get it right, no more disappointing Christmas mornings when I realize Santa's fucked it up yet again. I'm in line, so excited I'm standing on my tiptoes. Finally it's my turn. I scramble up into Santa's lap, he's ho-ho-hoing, and I start rattling off all the cool stuff I want when I notice there's something else in his lap, under his red Santa suit. And it's growing.

Santa' betting a hard-on while I'm sitting in his lap telling him all about the P.J. Sparkle doll I want for Christmas.

What could I do? Finished my list, hopped down, being careful not to touch Santa's rapidly expanding North Pole. I was five, Ethan. And you know what, to this day, still pisses me off? For years I thought I was special because I was the only kid Santa gave a hug to. Everyone else got a pat on the head but me, big old hug. From that moment on, my life has been absolute shit. Fucker didn't even bring me a P.J. Sparkle doll.

Juliet and this Guy Romeo
Don Zolidis

> Play
> Female
> 15
> Comic

> *Juliet has just woken from a fake death to discover Romeo, dead from inhaling too much Afrin.*

JULIET:

> Romeo? Where is Romeo?
> *(She spots him.)*
> WHAT THE CRAP?!
> *(JULIET searches his body.)*
> What's here? Afrin, closed in my true love's hand?
> Afrin, I see, hath been his timeless end:
> O churl! drunk all, and left no friendly drop
> To help me after? I will kiss thy lips;
> Haply some poison yet doth hang on them,
> To make die with a restorative.
> *(She touches his lips.)*
> Thy lips are warm.
> *(She takes out ROMEO's dagger.)*
> Oh happy dagger!
> *(She's about to stab herself, then talks to the audience.)*
> Then I was like, what the heck am I doing? Like how dumb is it to kill yourself over a guy, right? Especially a guy that like— you've known him for a week, and he's murdered two people. Like, talk about warning signs, right? So the first week of our relationship was great, he only killed two guys. We're hoping for three in our second week together. And basically, like, I didn't do anything wrong. And bonus – looks like I won't be marrying Paris. So that's cool.

Jump/Cut
Neena Beber

> Play
> Female
> 25-30
> Comic

Karen, a grad student, contemplates moving in with her boyfriend, Paul. This is not an easy decision. At. All.

KAREN:

I'm sorry, but I don't think moving in together is a see-how-it goes proposition. I think it's a turn my life upside-down, put my faith and my hope and my esteem in the hands of another human being, sacrifice my independence and my freedom and my self-sufficiency which I am willing to do on a leap, as an act of faith, an act of belief, but not as a dare or a gamble or a see-how-it-goes what-the-fuck…

(A pops of light. Karen faces us. To audience.) I always wanted to be one of those what-the-hell girls…you know the ones I mean… they usually have a little tattoo of, say, a dolphin on their ankle that they got on the spur of the moment when it was trendy, what the hell. They smoke cigs and drink too much, what the hell. They've all been with other women, even the straight ones, what the hell. They're sexy, despite their usually stringy hair and unmade-up faces, because they think they are, and they're young as shit, and skinny, and they live with this guy and then that guy without losing faith, or innocence, or pride, what the hell great way to save on rent and hey, it's fun for a while, cool and carefree and shit I am just not, have never been, carefree.

(A pop of light as Karen returns to the scene with Paul. To Paul.) I will move in with you, Paul, what the hell. Until I can find my own place at least. But I want you to know that I didn't ruin a romantic moment. It was more like a toaster-oven moment. A blender moment. A perfectly utilitarian non-moment. OK?

Let's Not Confuse the Situation
David-Matthew Barnes

Play
Female
17-25
Comic

Having been burned by bad relationships in the past, Janessa battles over her decision to give her new boyfriend, Colby, a key to her apartment.

JANESSA:

I was afraid that if I gave you a key to my apartment, you would freak out and run screaming from my life. I'm not always what men are looking for. You know the type. They want you to wear the right thing, cook all of their meals, keep a clean house. That's not who I am. Well, you know what I'm like. I like to live life moment by moment. I'm spontaneous. Maybe that's why I'm drawn to stand-up comedy. Do you think I would be good at it? *(Quick beat.)* I know my apartment isn't nearly as fancy as your townhouse. Once they get the rat problem under control here, this place could really be cozy. I'd really love to buy a house. My credit isn't what it used to be. I was young and foolish and I needed a lot of shoes. I went a little crazy with some credit cards. *(Beat.)* I changed my name. My real name is Tonya Carlisle. *(Quick beat.)* Would you like something to drink? I've got a two liter of Shasta in the freezer. Will that do? My ex-boyfriend and I were madly in love. *(Beat.)* Two months after we met, he decided to go back to his wife. I was devastated. *(Beat.)* She filed a restraining order against me. Isn't that crazy? *(Beat.)* Maybe it's time to put his picture away somewhere. I don't want you to feel uncomfortable. Especially since you have your own key now. I want you to feel like this apartment is yours, too.

Likeness

Katy Wix

> Freestanding monologue
> Female
> 20s-30s
> Comic

An artist's British model relishes her moment on the pedestal.

MODEL:

I took my earrings out. They made me look too frivolous.
Didn't sleep so well so be kind.
(She positions herself into a pose.)
Like this, yes?

Should I choose a point in the distance and fix my gaze? Speaking of gaze—I'm so glad you told me, really I am. I knew there was something else, some *one* else. I knew it. Suddenly now, it all makes complete sense. I mean, can you imagine if I'd actually fallen in love with you or something mad, like that? It all made so much sense when you told.

I don't know if you know this, but I have one eyebrow higher than the other. But if I do this face...then they even out. Shall I do that face? Do you want that?

There's an argument for lifting my arms up like this...but I suppose that's asking for trouble. Oh, what happens if I need the loo, which I will—my bladder goes off like a clock with a quarter chime.

I'm glad you told me. It's rare for me to be able talk about fabrics and things like that with men. Knew it was too good to be true. And the first time we kissed and you were so obsessed with my bum and now, honestly—I feel like the gods of hindsight are looking down and laughing at me.

Don't paint my nose too big, will you? Shall I hold something, for scale? That might help, like a tennis racket or something? I notice you're using a lot of blue. Are you going through a blue period, like Picasso?

Do you remember that time we followed Rufus Wainwright into a health food shop and we talked to him by the big bowl of strawberries and he told us he was looking for the strawberry of his dreams? He was staring at you. Just think, what could've been. I bet those same gods are laughing at you now. You probably could have shagged Rufus Wainwright, is my point, I guess.

Should I smile? No. No, I want to look arty.

Lost Love, The Final 100 Years #9

Peter Papadopoulos

> Play
> Female
> 20s-30s
> Comic

Tito is checking out Jan and Barb's bed, and Jan schools him on why he will not be living out the typical male fantasy she is sure he has in mind.

JAN:

Oh, right,
"Do you two girls mind if I watch you have sex?"
And this opportunity for voyeurism
is thankfully made possible by the fact that
we lesbians have sex all night every night
after every party
every picnic
every night club outing—
lesbians have sex constantly.
It's a fact!
Verified by B Hollywood movies
and porn sites
and Maxim Magazine:
lesbians
are forever DOING IT.
They never go to work
or vacuum dust bunnies out of the corners of their rooms
or lie in bed puking with the flu,
they just go to parties
in slinky dresses
with cool shaved legs
and then race home for hot sex.
And because we are lesbians
and don't have real feelings
sure, we don't mind having our sex
publicly
inviting you to watch

since it's not REAL sex anyways
it's just something fun and kinky
we do,
just a trendy game we're playing
to pass the time
before we go back to
screwing boys
and raising their fat, pasty kids.
NO, YOU CAN'T WATCH.

Love at 20
Neil LaBute

> Play
> Female
> 19
> Comic

Young Woman, just shy of 20, holds her cell phone in one hand, and wears a purse over the other shoulder.

YOUNG WOMAN:

This guy I'm seeing, well, he's my professor, actually, in this one history course—it's my second year at college, so that's cool—he's almost exactly 20 years older than me. Yep. "Twenty years your senior," my mom says, which is so gay because she's only, like, twenty-three years older than me, but she sounds like my grandma or something...She always says shit like that, but especially about him. My boyfriend. Well, I guess he's not actually that, technically, because he's got a wife and all that—no kids, though—and that's a bit of a bummer, but he's getting divorced, he totally is, but they just got a few things to work out. Legalities and all that crap and I've been very good about waiting for him. We started in together last semester—I'm only taking his "Empire Building from Napoleon to Nixon," because it fits my schedule and it's first thing in the morning, so he can give me a ride (my Honda is a piece of shit when it's cold)—but, yeah, we've been a couple for almost a year now, school year, anyway, and he's promised me that we're always going to be together. Forever. (Beat.) Well, until today, that is. Like 20 minutes ago...

Maytag Virgin
Audrey Cefaly

Play
Female
30s-40s
Comic

Lizzy, a woman from Alabama, compares her Christmas lawn ornamentation to her neighbor's display of the Virgin Mary.

LIZZY:

I told him straight up. Mr. Key. That is sinful idolatry. Even if it is the Virgin Mary. Then he pointed back at my yard and asked me about my Nativity and wasn't that the Virgin Mary right there by the manger, and I said, well, yes, it is, but she's not the 'focus.' She's a supporting character. You have a graven statue of Mary at the end of your driveway. Do you want to go to hell? God does not share his glory with another. Not even Jesus' mama, first commandment! He said that God never intended for us to take that literally and that the problem with protestants is that we don't know how to think for ourselves. Well now, was that a Christian thing to say? Then he brought up the topic of Carl Watkins two streets over with the flashing baby Jesus, which I had not seen…so of course I marched right over. And sure enough he was flashing…not the whole manger, just the Jesus. Lit up like some neon…like one of them vacancy signs at a cheap motel…ya know…born TODAY… born today. It didn't really say that but that's the message I got… born today.

Merry Cougar Christmas (#1)

Daniel Guyton

> Play
> Female
> 61-80
> Comic

Sylvia and Ethel have come to the mall to meet men. It turns out,
however, that Sylvia's tastes skew a bit young.

SYLVIA:

Not what you had in mind? So what did you have in mind,
Ethel? Little old lady stuff? Maybe we'd go out and buy a crochet-
ing needle? Perhaps a paisley yellow scarf to match your afghan?
Well I am sick and tired of being sick and tired, Ethel. I'm only as
old as I feel, and I feel like I'm 27. And I am going to live out the
rest of my days like I really am 27. Do you hear me? Now I know
you loved Ralph, Ethel. We all did. And I am so sorry that the
cancer took him the way it did. Lord knows he took better care of
himself than you and I ever did. But he's dead. And for whatever
reason, God has seen fit to keep us alive. Can you see the irony
in that Ethel? Alive! So you can choose to look this gift horse in
the mouth if you want to, but I am going to live. And I'll be hot-
damned if I'm going to go out and find another man whose foot is
halfway into the grave as well as mine is. I want someone young
and vibrant, who reminds me that life is for the living, and death
is for everyone else. Do you hear me? Now what about you? Are
you gonna live, Ethel, or are you gonna spend another Christmas
Eve all by your lonesome, crying about Ralph?

Merry Cougar Christmas (#2)
Daniel Guyton

Play
Female
61-80
Comic

Sylvia and Ethel have come to the mall to meet men. It turns out, however, that Sylvia's tastes skew a bit young. And no wonder. She has taken a page from her deceased husband's playbook.

SYLVIA:

George had seven mistresses over the course of our marriage. Did you know that? I knew about one of the girls at the time, but… after he died, three of them showed up at his funeral. Another two sent flowers. I finally asked his secretary how many there were in total, including herself, unfortunately. And…well…after a great deal of arguing, and a…threat of mutilation with a jewel-encrusted letter opener, she told me seven. I am convinced she was telling me the truth. And do you know how old the oldest of these women was, Ethel? Thirty-four years old. And that was eight years after they had broken up. George was sixty-nine at the time of death. And you think that *my* behavior is appalling?
(She points to the boys around her.)
I finally understand why he did it though. The vibrancy of youth. It's like a drug. The elixir of life. It makes me feel immortal, if I can be completely honest. And I've discovered something magical through all of this, Ethel, which has helped me out immensely. George did not sleep with younger women because of *me*. He did it because he was afraid of death.

A Midsummer Night's Dream (#1)

William Shakespeare

> Play
> Female
> 25-40
> Comic

Titania wakes, and under Oberon's spell, falls hopelessly in love with Bottom, upon whom Puck has fixed a donkey's head.

TITANIA:

Out of this wood do not desire to go:
Thou shalt remain here, whether thou wilt or no.
I am a spirit of no common rate;
The summer still doth tend upon my state;
And I do love thee: therefore, go with me;
I'll give thee fairies to attend on thee,
And they shall fetch thee jewels from the deep,
And sing while thou on pressed flowers dost sleep;
And I will purge thy mortal grossness so
That thou shalt like an airy spirit go.
Peaseblossom! Cobweb! Moth! and Mustardseed!
    (…)
Be kind and courteous to this gentleman;
Hop in his walks and gambol in his eyes;
Feed him with apricocks and dewberries,
With purple grapes, green figs, and mulberries;
The honey-bags steal from the humble-bees,
And for night-tapers crop their waxen thighs
And light them at the fiery glow-worm's eyes,
To have my love to bed and to arise;
And pluck the wings from Painted butterflies
To fan the moonbeams from his sleeping eyes:
Nod to him, elves, and do him courtesies.

Mill Town Girls
Audrey Cefaly

Play
Female
20s-40s
Comic

Betty, a Southerner, discovers that Mr. Autrey has been secretly monitoring conversations in the teachers' lounge.

BETTY:

Well. I can now confirm with an almost arrogant degree of certainty that Principal Autrey has been secretly monitoring our conversations in the teacher's lounge. He has been listening in over the PA system—something I have suspected for quite some time—but I now have proof!! On Tuesday, Janette Mullins and I were having our coffee break between 2nd and 3rd and she confided in me that she would like to take the winter off to have her 2nd child but she was worried about whether her job would still be around. And that's when I told her that I had gone past Jimmy's office earlier that day and had found a memo on his desk that was over 7 years old. And when in the world was he ever going to clean up that mountain of papers off of his desk. And the very next day, I walked by his office again, and don't you know, that desk was clean as a whistle. Proves nothing right? Well, it gets better. I told Janette about my little discovery and she just wouldn't believe it. And that's when we decided to conduct a little experiment. So then last week during our little break I said to her "Janette, do you ever wonder why Jimmy parts his hair on the left side like that?" And she said, "Why no, V, I hadn't ever wondered that." And I said, "Well, I do, I wonder it all the time. Do you reckon he would look better if he parted on the right?" And she said, "Well, I don't know, I reckon he might." And I said, "I do, I really do, and I think I might like to see that. In fact, I think it might make him look 10 years younger, what do you think Janette?" And she said, "Well, V, he is a man of fashion, perhaps we shouldn't question such things."

The *very* next day. Parted on the right! Bastard!

The Monologue Show (From Hell) (#2)
Don Zolidis

Play
Female
Teen
Comic

Alyssa and Taylor Swift are BFFs.

ALYSSA:

Isn't it funny how the voices in your head talk to you some-times? I have two, actually. My first one, my favorite one, is Taylor Swift. I know, right? Cra-zy. It is so great having Taylor Swift in my head though. She's always like, "you are a strong woman, and don't you forget it." I love her. It's like she's sitting on my shoulder and saying things like "Shake it off" all the time. It's magical. (…)

But sometimes I worry that Taylor is getting bored, because, you know, I'm just like an ordinary person, right? I'm not like some big fancy star or whatever. And I know she says nice things about my clothes but she's probably thinking like, "no one even designed this, I can't believe you're wearing it. This is from The Gap. Who wears clothes from the Gap?"

So that's when I like to thrill her. So this one time I went to Macy's, and I was like, "Taylor, what would you do if I shoplifted this sweater right now?" And Taylor Swift got all worried and she was like, "don't shoplift," and I was like okay, so instead I went to the counter, and there was this nice lady there, and she was like, can I help you? And I made my eyes go all crazy and then I faked hav-ing a gun and I was like "GIVE ME ALL THE MONEY NOW!!"

OMG, Taylor was freaking out, it was so funny! So I tied up the lady with a scarf or whatever and I grabbed the cash and I was like, "RUN!" and there's this security guard chasing me—and I just grabbed this mannequin and smashed him over the head with it? Boom. He's like unconscious and bleeding or whatever and this alarm sounds like WEE-OO WEE-OO, it was so fun. Taylor was not bored. She's screaming her little Taylor Swift scream and let me tell you, it still sounded beautiful. She is an angel. We get in my car, and there's that little mall security vehicle chasing us—it's like a Smartcar or whatever, like three feet long—I floor it, smash headfirst into it, and I'm like screaming, "I AM INSANE! DO NOT MESS WITH ME!" It was hilarious, the security guard was crying or whatever. He's like "I have kids and a family!" Then I tear out of there before the cops show up. I told Taylor, I am never going to let you be bored with me. And I think she really liked that.

She's going to be so surprised by what I do next. Ha ha ha ha.

Mr. Perfect
William Missouri Downs

> Play
> Female
> 20s
> Comic

On a flight over Kansas, Zooey, a quirky and sexy flight attendant, meets Jeffrey, the voice-actor who's narrated most of her pulp fiction fantasy audiobooks. Before initiating him into the Mile-High Club, she tells him how she wants it, wink wink.

ZOEY:

You can't blame a girl for wanting more. (…) I want to know that you'll call tomorrow. That we'll date for an appropriate amount of time, maybe three to five chapters. And then at the end of chapter six, you'll take me out to dinner and surprise me with a ring. In chapters seven through fourteen we'll rise above the normal humdrum of existence. We'll also survive that tragic night in chapter nine when your mother dies in that awful train wreck. In chapter ten, our love will rise above my momentary fling with a handsome priest named Father Ralph who has been sent into exile at a remote parish for insulting a bishop. Despite the fact that he's sworn to a life of celibacy, he breaks his vows, consummates our passion, and dies of a broken heart. But you forgive my wandering spirit and together we raise the love child as our own. Years later, in chapter eighteen, on my deathbed, with our children and love children gathered around us, the music will crest and I'll know that we've found our purpose and lived a life worthy of a soundtrack. (…)

I want fantasy, romanticism and pulp fiction rolled into one. I don't want kitchen sink realism—I want realism where the sink flies. I want, before we begin, to hold a comfortable story in my hands, to hit play and know that there's something or someone in the control booth—someone who thought things through. But most of all I want *climax*. No story is complete without *climax*. *(Sexy:)* Know what I mean…*climax?*

Mr. Right
Jonathan Joy

Freestanding monologue
Female
17-25
Comic

Denise is a small town girl with a heart of gold and a head of air.

DENISE:

Mom never likes any of the guys I date, but you're not supposed to judge a book by its cover. That's what the Bible says.

Anyway, how was I supposed to know that Alan was on that sex offender list or that Sam would go on to rob that Speedway when the cigarette tax went through the roof? They both seemed like perfectly nice guys.

Well, I've met somebody new and he's different. Got a real good job, too. His name is Marco and he's real sweet on me and he's just gorgeous. He's got this long dark wavy hair and a thick black beard and beautiful olive skin. He looks a lot like Jesus if Jesus was Italian…and had really big beautiful muscles.

Marco works as an importer and exporter of precious cargo going to and from all kinds of places in South America. When he's in town, we get to drive all over the place delivering packages to people. It's real top secret. He doesn't like me to talk about it. He got real mad once when I tried to look inside one of them boxes. He said those boxes got medicine in them and he's delivering that medicine to people in need. I thought that was real nice of him and then I thought he's kind of like a doctor in a way. And he helps people in real bad neighborhoods, too, which is something that I don't think a lot of doctors do.

It's nice to finally meet a guy that has a real future ahead of him. Mom'll love him.

Naomi in the Living Room

Christopher Durang

> Play
> Female
> 40s+
> Comic

A living room. Enter Naomi, followed by John and Johanna, an attractive young couple. Naomi, though, looks odd. She plants herself somewhere definitive—by the mantelpiece, for instance—and gestures toward the room.

NAOMI:

And this is the living room. And you've seen the dining room, and the bedroom, and the bathroom. (…) The dining room is where we dine. The bedroom is where we go to bed. The bathroom is where we take a bath. The kitchen is where we…cook. That doesn't sound right. The kitchen is where we…collect kitsch. Hummel figurines, Statue of Liberty salt and pepper shakers, underpants that say Home of the Whopper, and so on. Kitsch. The kitchen is where we look at kitsch. The laundry room is where we do laundry. And the living room is where Hubert and I do all of our living. Our major living. So that's the living room. (…) We use the cellar to… we go to the cellar to…replenish our cells. We go to the attic to …practice our tics, our facial tics. (*Her face consorts variously.*) And we go to the carport, to port the car. Whew! Please don't ask me any more questions, I'm afraid I may not have the strength to find the answers. (*Laughs uproariously*) Please, sit down, don't let my manner make you uncomfortable. Sit on one of the sitting devices, we use them for sitting in the living room.

> *(There is a couch and one chair to choose from. JOHN and JO-HANNA go to sit on the couch.)*

(*Screams at them.*) DON'T SIT THERE, I WANT TO SIT THERE!!! (…) No, no, sit down. Please, make yourselves at home, this is the living room, it's where Rupert and I do all our living.

New in the Motherhood

Lisa Loomer

>Play
>Female
>20s-30s
>Comic

A new-ish mom joins some other moms in the park. Still...trying to figure the whole "mom thing" out...

MOM:

Oh hi. This bench taken? *(Sits.)* Cool.

(Sees son, calls out; lightly.) Put it down, Harry. Down, babe. The tricycle is a means of *transportation*.

(Laughs.) He's three. Everything's a penis.

(She takes out a cigarette.) God, I hate the park. If anyone had told me I'd be sentenced to five to ten years in the park...I'd have stuck with a cat.

(Re: cigarette.) Oh, this is clove by the way. *(Takes a drag.)* All right, it's not clove, but it's the park. See, the park for me is like...Dante's Purgatory. Not Dante's Inferno— that'd be exciting, you'd meet interesting people...But, I mean, day after day of whose turn is it on the swing? Couldn't we just let 'em duke it out? I mean, I used to go to an office...Like—in a building? I was a type A personality! Okay, B minus, but still...

(Takes a drag; smiles.) Look, I know he's a boy, you gotta take 'em outside. They *will not* play Scrabble. They'll throw the pieces at the cat. And they won't miss 'cause they're boys.

(Lightly.) And you can't just let his dad take him to the park, cause, hey—"Where was Mom? Working?" He'll be in therapy the rest of his life—

(Notices; matter of fact.) Harry? No, honey—put the little girl down. Put her down, babe.

(Waits; easy.) Put her down and use your words, Harry.

(Beat.) Not *those* words—

(Laughs.) Hey, remind me to cancel Showtime—!

Nice Tie
Rich Orloff

> Play
> Female
> 26–40
> Comic

A woman nurses a drink. A man walks up to the bar, and asks to buy her a drink.

WOMAN:

Oh, I don't know. First you buy me a drink, and then we get to chatting, and if we're not too bored with each other, you ask for my phone number, and I figure what the hell, so I give it to you. If you don't call me, I'm disappointed. If you do call me, we go out, and either I don't like you, or I like you and you don't like me. And I'm disappointed. Or we do like each other, and we go out some more, and things become pretty wonderful—great sex, revealing conversations, compatible neuroses—but I discover I want more than you can give. And I'm disappointed.

Or we stay with it, and we get closer and closer and more in love and more dependent on each other, which gives us the strength to go through periods of emotional turmoil, mutual doubts, and things said in anger that we'll pretend to forget but which will come up again during the post-natal depression I'll have after the birth of our first child. *If* we get married, that is, and Lord knows how many friends I'll lose because they like me but they're just not comfortable around you.

After our second child, the unresolved conflicts we buried for the sake of our marriage will propel you into a torrid affair, either with someone you work with or, God forbid, one of my few friends who *is* comfortable around you. I'll try to forgive you, eventually, and either you'll resent the obligation of a monogamous relationship, or you'll try to become philosophical about it, by which point both our children will be in intensive therapy.

The divorce will be ugly, expensive, and years later than it should've been. I'll never be able to trust men again, those who aren't frightened off by my sagging features and two sadomasochistic children. The kids'll blame me, of course, and I'll die all alone.

I think I'll pass on the drink. It's a nice offer, but the pain just isn't worth it.

The Norwegians (#1)

C. Denby Swanson

> Play
> Female
> 30s-40s
> Comic

Betty, a transplant from Kentucky, explains the term "Minnesota nice" to Olive, who is from Texas.

BETTY:

Here in Minnesota, you gotta find a lover before the first freeze or else it's just too late, you're iced in for a very long time, all alone. They don't tell you that when you move here, but it's true. You are iced in for all the short days, there are so many short days before the sun comes back and it begins to thaw. Short days and long nights. Long cold nights all alone, just the sound of the radiator in your apartment turning on, the knocking and the whispering of steam. Just leftover soup heated up mid-afternoon before the light fades. In fact, you make so much borscht that your poop turns red and you think it's blood and you have to have a tube with a camera on it shoved up your ass. On camera. In February. And the doctor aims the tube at you and says, "Here we go!" and then you watch your looming butt cheeks docked like the international space station by a tiny camera on a tube, like the space shuttle, right there on TV. It's that kind of cold, Olive. It's the cold of those bulky purple and yellow sweaters that you have to put on to take out the garbage, so that you're shapeless, like a big purple and yellow potato. That's you: a big plate of starch. You're just purple and yellow and shapeless and starchy, and you've just had a camera up your ass. On TV. Unless of course you find a lover, and hold on to him, and you make your own steam, and knocking, and whispering, and you feed each other food from your hands, not soup but solid food, and you draw lines with ice cubes down each other's body, no one's cold then. No one's cold. No one's alone. So did you do that, Olive? Did you find someone before it froze? No. Oh, you tried, now, didn't you. But you failed. You didn't get a lover. No. No, you didn't. Because he left you. He froze you out. He left you to die.

(OLIVE sobs.)

That is Minnesota nice, my new little friend. What I just did to you. That's what Minnesota nice feels like in your heart after five years. Five winters. That's all it takes.

The Norwegians (#2)
C. Denby Swanson

Play
Female
30s-40s
Comic

Betty, a transplant from Kentucky, stands in a pool of light. She's waiting, on edge, ready for something. She is in Minnesota. It's cold. And she has hired someone to kill her fiancé.

BETTY:

The Norwegians. And their Lutheran Church. Home of orphan and refugee relocation services all over the world. Their revered social services. Fuck me. Fuck them. The Norwegians and their gravlax. Does anyone even know what that is? An alien word for, I don't know, something fish-like. And fermented trout. Fermented. Trout. And lutefisk—fish steeped in lye and then covered in ashes. I mean, my god, fish, lye and ashes. Fish, Lye & Ashes. It sounds like a band name from the 1970's. Like, a white R&B band. And their perpetually cheerful snow suits and their stupid local customs. They will stop in any weather and help a stranger change their tire. I just want to scream at them, I know you don't really mean that. You cannot love people who make gravlax. You cannot love people who make lutefisk. You cannot FUCK people who make elderberry wine, not an actual fuck, not a true heartfelt beautiful intimate fuck, as I discovered. Late. Or lingonberries. Lingonberries. If that doesn't bring up dirty images in your head, I don't know what would. What lover would let you serve them lingonberries? And my god, hotdish: meat and Stovetop drenched in mushroom soup and covered in tater tots. That's not even—that's like casserole death. But Norwegians hand this "food" out in the neighborhood when new people move in. When there are pot lucks. They think hotdish is welcoming. They think lingonberries are—Well. These are fearful, terrifying, terrible, very frightening things to serve people.

(She checks her phone. Nothing.) If I could have hired him to kill himself, it would be over by now.

(She pulls a baseball hat down low over her face.)

The Outrageous Adventures of Sheldon & Mrs. Levine
Sam Bobrick and Julie Stein

> Play
> Female
> 50s
> Comic

Mrs. Levine responds to her thirty-one-year old son's letter, in which he calls her a lunatic.

MRS. LEVINE:

(Softly.) Lunatic! Lunatic!

(She takes a deep breath. Her anger builds.) Well Sheldon, maybe I am a lunatic. Maybe you have to be to survive in today's world. How sane do you really want to be knowing we live in a world where the ice caps are melting, the ozone layer is disintegrating and the banks don't give away free toasters anymore? How much stability is healthy when we know we have to live with dirty air, acid rain and fruit that rots in your grocery bag before you get home? Doesn't it bother you, my dear son, that the meat they sell us is so full of steroids, the cows could play basketball for the Knicks? Doesn't it burn your ass, dear Sheldon, that those sleaze-ball politicians we elect to take care of us, all have better retirement and medical plans than we do? (…) And everywhere you go people giving you the finger. My landlord, my paperboy and that nun I sometimes sit next to on the bus…You want to know why? Because the world is full of people wound so tight that any minute they can snap like a pretzel. Sanity, Sheldon? Why? What's the point? Let me tell you kiddo, if one morning you wake up and you're not a lunatic, there's something seriously wrong with you.

Overruled (#1)
George Bernard Shaw

Play
Female
20s-30s
Comic

Mrs. Lunn, weary of being pursued, responds to Mr. Juno's romantic overture in a way he does not expect.

MRS. LUNN:

There you go, like all the rest of them! I ask you, how do you expect a woman to keep up what you call her sensibility when this sort of thing has happened to her about three times a week, ever since she was seventeen? It used to upset me and terrify me at first. Then I got rather a taste for it. It came to a climax with Gregory: that was why I married him. Then it became a mild lark, hardly worth the trouble. After that I found it valuable once or twice as a spinal tonic when I was run down; but now it's an unmitigated bore. I don't mind your declaration: I daresay it gives you a certain pleasure to make it. I quite understand that you adore me; but (if you don't mind) I'd rather you didn't keep on saying so.

Patience & Hannah

Gabrielle Sinclair

> Play
> Female
> 17-25
> Comic

It's night, and Hannah is a long way from home. She is to be married in only a few hours. She talks with her friend, Patience.

HANNAH:

I have reason to believe that Eric, my perfect fiancé might… he might…you see, he might just be…a pillow. *(Beat.)* See—Patience —listen—please—please! I have these Really Great Friends. And they threw me the *best* showers. Christmas, Kitchen, Bonnet showers. But, Patience—a very big and very growing part of me knows—*knows*—that I told my friends I was engaged to someone really supportive who made me feel comforted and loved, but then, when they met him they saw, they saw he was, in fact, not a man, but a hypoallergenic body pillow, the kind I always wanted—yes from Macy's—and that they see the truth, but I can't see it, I have no idea, and so they just sort of decided as a group not to say anything. They just threw all these bridal showers and these brunches and just let it happen. But I don't *want* to marry a pillow, Patience! I don't want to have a pillow's babies. I don't. Even if he is my soul mate.

Phone Arts
L.B. Hamilton

Play
Female
40s-50s
Comic

Jane, a woman of color, homemaker and "phone artist," defends her work to her partner, Moire. As for Moire, she's dubious.

JANE:

Listen, Moire...I'm good. I found my path. I am a performance artist! (...) I have instincts, Sweetie. And a following. I know what they need even when they don't. I can talk whole new worlds for them and take them where they never knew they could go. I can make them laugh; I can make them cry; and they are in a big new place and are..are...transformed. And they come back for more—it's a built-in market with huge return business! And they don't have to dress up and go somewhere and hang out with a bunch of snooty strangers to find art—No...it's right there, at their fingertips. And my art can't be stolen from them and it won't be ruined by time, or lose value, because mine is a living art—always.. always...um...reinventing itself! Yeah! Powerful and, and...um... and empowering! (...)

It's in your face, real..um...audiophonic! Yeah! Audiophonic art. Oh think about it, Sweetie. We could branch out. Make a fortune, buy a house—have that baby?

Pick

Katy Wix

> Freestanding monologue
> Female
> 30s-50s
> Comic

Pandora, a British woman, laments her name.

PANDORA:

(…) God, how I longed to be a Jess, or a Sarah or even something devastating like Brittney. But when the teachers called out 'Pandora in the playground, only one person turned their head to see, and that was me. There were no others.

It's been a burden, my whole life, my name. And you may think that a name doesn't really matter, *that* much, but it does! What's even worse is that it didn't even suit me. A Pandora should be elegant, serene. I was fat and shy. It's so much worse, like being an ugly Belle, a quiet Gabby, or a clumsy Grace. Some little girls are desperate to stand out, aren't they, and be noticed, actively looking for signs of their uniqueness, but that wasn't me—I was desperate not to be seen. There was nothing you could throw over the name Pandora to try and conceal it, no chance of pushing it into a corner and hoping no one would notice. I was furious with my parents for forcing me into the middle of the room for all to see...because they named me Pandora. Nominative determinism. Your name affects your future. Because no one called Gary will ever run the country.

And then, when I got a bit older, the boys would make really lame jokes about my box. Well, by then I knew the myth quite well and I would say, "Actually, that's a complete misnomer. Pandora opened a *jar*, but it's often mistranslated as a 'box', and besides, she only opened it out of curiosity; she didn't mean any harm and anyone else would have done exactly the same, if they had been in her position."

So, this woman, this poor woman Pandora—created by the gods, has been the victim of victim-blaming. It was Prometheus's fault quite honestly. So there we go—who was really to blame—a man. This defenseless woman has taken all this blame—a disproportionate amount of blame—when really Prometheus started it. All Pandora ever did was open a jar, like Nigella—she has been completely misrepresented. (…)

Pilfering Rome
Jonathan Joy

Play
Female
26-40
Comic

*Lulu, a strong-willed Appalachian woman as likely to drink anyone
under the table as she is to make the best chicken and dumplings
this side of Bob Evans, explains the "situation" on the porch.*

LULU:

It ain't the first time a man been tied up-tight with a garden hose in
our front yard, and I'm sure it won't be the last.

(Pause.) Milo came home a little soused last night when your
mother was trying to catch up on a week's worth of her stories. Now
I love Milo, you know that, but I wasn't in the mood for anything
exceptin' to find out whether Luke had realized yet that his new
wife was really his arch enemy Alexander come back from the dead
and after a sex change, but Milo kept talking about "the game" and
trying to get all cuddly with me, but it was Saturday night and he
knows good and well that you leave a Lulu alone on a Saturday
night. We got six other nights a week for hanky panky, thank you.
Well, except Monday, 'cause 'a Monday Night Raw. Anyway, five
nights…point is, he wasn't taking no for an answer, so I had to put
an exclamation mark on it. That's why he's knocked out and tied
up to our porch. *(Pause.)* Any questions?

Protocol
Bara Swain

> Play
> Female
> 20s-30s
> Comic

In a hotel room in Mallorca, Spain, Mary speaks to Robert who is asleep on the couch.

MARY:

OH MY GOD, ROBERT. My mother phoned last night— (*Rolls eyes.*) again!…from the new Westside Market on the East Side. Which really bothers me, you know? Isn't that like calling the South Pole the new North Pole? And I thought to myself, "Thank you, Alexander Graham Bell. If it weren't for you, my mother and I couldn't debate the nutritional value of Chicken Asparagus Roll-ups versus Broccoli-Cheese Casserole," which, in the long run doesn't matter anyway because the kids won't eat anything green except for seedless grapes and mint chocolate chip ice-cream. (*SHE laughs.*) I know, I know, I know. I told her, firmly, I said, "Mother, do not call me unless it's an emergency. Please. That's why it's called "vacation," am I right or am I wrong?

(*MARY positions ROBERT so that SHE can lie in his lap. SHE places his arm around her. His dead weight arm keeps falling down.*) Anyway, I was trying to catch the waiter's eye for a second spicy pork tapas order and another frozen margarita—(*sits back up*) – you were on your fourth and, Honey, I could hear you yelling, "BRAIN FREEZE! BRAIN FREEZE!" all the way from the men's room to the bar. And all of a sudden I hear the Star Spangled Banner playing inside my purse. It was an out-of-body experience, Robert! (*Singing.*) Oh, say can you see? (*Speaking*). Inside my purse, the national anthem is playing, in the middle of the night—(*Singing*) "by the dawn's early light"—(*Speaking.*) 4,000 miles away from the Hudson River to the middle of the Mediterranean Sea… (*Proudly.*) which I can spell, by the way…in the middle of a local bar, where half the staff look like the school crossing guard at PS 334.

(*SHE lies down, then sits upright quickly.*) And, P.S., that's called an observation, Robert, not a judgment. I am not passing judgment. If I were in Korea, half the staff would look like Hae-Won, my manicurist. (*MARY shows ROBERT her fingernails, then looks at them, too.*) OH BOY OH BOY OH BOY, I need a manicure. Maybe we can include that in our itinerary today, Robert. I <u>love</u> that word. I-tin-er-ar-y. (*Pleased.*) It doesn't rhyme with anything. Like the word "orange."

Quake (#3)
Melanie Marnich

Play
Female
30s
Comic

Lucy and a Nice Man are on a date. The Nice Man is very animated—talking, laughing, sipping wine, nodding in agreement, etc.—but completely silent. Lucy goes through the motions of the date, interacting with him, but speaks her thoughts.

LUCY:

Uh huh. Good sense of humor. Personal hygienic all right. Solid hairline.

(He laughs with his mouth open.)

Three fillings. one crown. Not bad. Nice hands. Masculine. Good sign. Note: Do laundry. Out of shampoo. Itch. *(She scratches.)* Focus, focus.

(She nods with him.)

Actually…Nice smile. Nice eyes. No. Wait. Great eyes. Dreamy eyes. Yeah. And smart. Really smart. Generous. Kind. Supportive. Sweet. Stable. Romantic. Good to me. Nice to me. Oooo. Likes me. Could like him. Could kiss him. French. Snuggle. Spoon. Sweet. Faithful. Dependable. Loyal. Irish setter. Cocker spaniel. Trapped. Stuck. Rut. Help. Panic. Escape. Move. Move. Move.

(LUCY leaves.)

Quiche Isn't Sexy
Gabriel Davis

> Play
> Female
> 17-25
> Comic

A young woman is disappointed in her dinner, and consequently, her date.

YOUNG WOMAN:

Quiche isn't sexy. It's pretentious. Quiche is an egg trying to be more than breakfast. It's an omelet disguising itself as a savory pie. It's the perky beginning to one's day when it should be the lusty end.

You could have made a rack of lamb, rare and wonderful. Small bites would turn to large bites and soon we'd have the lamb bones in our hands and we'd be devouring it. After, we'd devour each other.

Lamb is delicious and impossible not to devour…you can't help yourself. You feel… almost starved as you first approach. You try to start slow but something drives you to go faster and faster and you don't care if you get covered in juices and flesh because you're…well, you're not eating a Quiche.

A Quiche is eaten in tiny, dainty bites. One does not devour a Quiche. And by serving me a Quiche, you are telling me something.

That's why, as sweet as this Quiche is…it's the pretense of a romantic dinner. It's two children kissing on the lips and exchanging promise rings. An egg is basically immature chicken. We haven't hatched, you see. We've tried.

But neither you, nor I are interested in what you've put on the menu.

The Rehearsal (#1)

Don Zolidis

> Play
> Female
> Teen
> Comic

A young teacher tries to pull off a production of Guys and Dolls, *but putting a musical together is never easy, especially with this crew. But it's in her choreography for "A Bushel and a Peck" that Deb truly distinguishes herself.*

DEB:

All right—this came to me in a dream—we all dress up like chickens. With like feathers and stuff—and then we make a bunch of high-pitched squeals like this—"eeeeee!" and then we do some clucking. And then it's like—
(She starts a very strange version of the chicken dance while singing a few lines from "A Bushel and a Peck.")
Strut strut strut peck peck peck there's birdseed over there right? Like we just spread birdseed all over the stage—and we're just like eating it, right? That's part of the dance. And then it's like "Oh no! Here comes the farmer! Run for your lives!" And then we all run around with another one of the "eeeeees"! And the we gather ourselves, right? Kill the Farmer. Kill the Farmer. So Adelaide sings —
(She sings another line from "A Bushel and a Peck.")
We're just like—death to the farmer! And I want you, you, and you—just grab him, right? And now we're peck peck pecking out his eyes—And then when he's dead we feast on his innards.
(Short pause.)
It's a metaphor for love.
(They all look at her.)
It's a director's concept.

The Rehearsal (#2)

Don Zolidis

> Play
> Female
> Teen
> Comic

A young teacher tries to pull off a production of Guys and Dolls, *but putting a musical together is never easy, especially when your lead would rather be in* Wicked. *At the first rehearsal, Morgan tries with limited success to make the best of a disappointing situation.*

MORGAN:

Hi everyone! You know me! I'm Morgan Hill, and I'll be playing the part of Miss Sarah Brown, which is the second most fun part in the play, next to the other lead, Adelaide. I don't mind, though, because I really like wearing starchy costumes and having my hair in a bun. And also awesome! I get to kiss Barry in this show, which I've really been looking forward to for a while because that's totally what I think I'd be doing with my life at this point! Not that I'm bitter! I'm not bitter! I love my part! I love singing really high and showing no emotion on stage! By the way, I wanted to do *Wicked*, which is an incredibly awesome show and I would have made the best Elphaba ever—can I just do a little bit of my audition song? (…)

But that's cool. Apparently, we don't have the right to do that show or something—so instead we're doing this show, which is just great, which is awesome, cause instead of flying and singing amazing songs, I get to be Miss Sarah Brown—who is working for the Salvation Army, can you believe that?! How much fun is it to work for the Salvation Army and ring that bell! Much more fun than flying and using magic, I can tell you that much! And I think this is the year that Barry learned what deodorant was, so that's a bonus! And it looks like some of his pimples are clearing up, double bonus! I can't wait to do this show!!!! *(She takes a deep breath.)* I am a team player.

Same Old
Stephanie Caldwell

> Freestanding monologue
> Female
> 30s-50s
> Comic

Ruby, a colorful "life stylist" and relationship coach, offers her friend some tips on writing the best online dating profile.

RUBY:

So, darling, when you go to write your profile, here's what I want you to remember: I want you to think of your answer to each question as if you're pulling back a curtain, o-o-opening that curtain just a teensy peek to reveal a brief...glimpse...of who you are. And...then...the curtain closes. Next question... another peek... oooh, something very different and VERY intriguing! And...the curtain closes. Next question: you get the idea. The key here is not to be exhaustive and literal; don't aim for a clear and honest portrait. No, no, no! Instead aim for a tantalizing pastiche, an impressionistic mélange. More Monet, less Manet. More Picasso, less Singer Sargent. Observe:

What I'm Doing with My Life: Creating beauty where there is none and urging a little chaos where it's needed, etc., etc.

I'm Really Good At: Balancing on one foot. Improvising Moroccan cuisine. Sounding like just about anyone I choose, etc., etc., (You see?)

Six Things I Could Never Do Without: Salt. Air. Wi-Fi. Ras al Hanout. An abacus. Sequins.

You see? Isn't this fun? Wouldn't you want to message me? I'd want to message me! Now you try...

I Spend a Lot of Time Thinking About....?

Second Lady
M. Kilburg Reedy

> Play
> Female
> 40s-50s
> Comic

Mrs. Erskine is a politician's wife. Her husband is running for Vice-President. In the middle of a political address, she loses it.

MRS. ERSKINE:

(She picks up the beginning of her speech, puts on her glasses, and reads.) "The League of Women Voters can provide the leadership needed to develop the National Community. Throughout your history you have met each challenge of the cause of democracy. I offer you another challenge, perhaps the greatest one you have yet faced."

(She puts down her glasses, then cracks up laughing.) I could just about die of embarrassment saying things like that. I can hardly keep from blushing sometimes. *(Becoming quite giddy.)* Do you want to know the funniest thing about it? I happen to know that this speech was originally written for the Rotarians. My husband just inserted "League of Women Voters" wherever "Rotary Club" appeared. Were you feeling flattered and pleased to know that you have consistently "met each challenge of the cause of democracy?" Sad to say, those glowing words of praise were never meant for you at all.

(Turns to photos behind her.) I don't know how they keep a straight face. I really don't. And they all do it, you see, all those men. Republicans do it more than Democrats—they seem to be born with a nose for the historical impact of a phrase. But most Democrats pick it up, too, after they've been around for a while, and they start to talk just the same. Even Joseph will sometimes say things to me in a tone of voice that makes me think he is half expecting me to write it all down. He gets this very intense look in his eyes, and he'll say something like: "I'm going to change the face of this country's social welfare system." It makes me want to look around the room to see if anyone else is there. (…)

I get the feeling sometimes that I'm there to be a witness. That I'm supposed to carry his private words and deeds with me until it's time to pass them on to posterity. *(On "posterity," she throws a paper airplane she has constructed from the first page of her speech.)*

Seduction and Snacks
Tara Sivec

Novel
Female
20s
Comic

Claire has strong opinions on motherhood.

CLAIRE:

Is it me or does it seem like you're in the middle of a horrible Alcoholics Anonymous meeting whenever someone finds out you never want children? Should I stand up, greet the room as a whole, and confess what brings me to the seventh circle of Hell I constantly find myself in? It's a house of horrors where pregnant women asking me to touch their protruding bellies and have in-depth discussions about their vaginas surround me. They don't understand why the words placenta and afterbirth should never be used in a sentence. Ever; especially over coffee in the middle of the day.

You know what brought me to the decision? The video we saw in health class in sixth grade. The one set back in the seventies that had some woman screaming bloody murder with sweat dripping off of her face while her husband lovingly patted her forehead with a towel and told her she was doing great. Then the camera panned down to the crime scene between her legs: the blood, the goo, the gore, and the humungous porn bush that now had a tiny little head squeezing its way out. (…) From that moment on, my motto was: I'm never having children.

"So, Claire, what do you want to be when you grow up?"

"I'm never having children."

"Claire, did you choose a major yet?"

"I'm never having children."

"Would you like fries with that?

"I'm never having children."

Of course there are always those in your life who think they can change your mind. (…)

Then you have the people who believe your flippancy is due to some deep, dark, secret issue with your uterus (…).

The simple truth is, I just never thought pushing a tiny human out of me which turns my vagina into something resembling roast beef that no man would ever want to look at, let along bang, was a stellar idea. End of story.

Shooting Star (#1)
Steven Dietz

> Play
> Female
> 40s-50s
> Comic

Elena, fairly happy with herself, spots an old flame in an airport and tries to get his attention by not getting his attention.

ELENA:

I wanted to be doing something interesting, something of import, when he first saw me. I didn't want to be just another bored, wrinkled, embittered traveler waiting in line to buy a candy bar and a *Cosmo.* (I'd already done that, they were in my bag.) I wanted to be doing something unique, appealing…(*Holds her waist in*) and possibly *thinning.*

So, I sat on the floor. Took off my shoes. And I began to meditate. In my lotus, near the windows, overlooking the snow-covered planes.

With my closed eye, I envisioned inner light and world peace and aeronautic tranquility.

With my slightly open other eye, I kept a lookout.

Where was he? Did he leave? Did he not see me and leave? Or: Did he see me and leave?!

Light peace and tranquility were put on hold as I de-lotused and sort of *crawled* behind a row of open chairs—to a place where I could spy from.

I peeked my head up and looked.

He was gone.

Okay. Well. *That certainly played out to perfection.*

Shooting Star (#2)
Steven Dietz

> Play
> Female
> 40s-50s
> Comic

> *Elena runs into an old flame in the airport, and he admits that he has thought about her from time to time, when he listens to NPR, which was her favorite station.*

ELENA:

THAT'S what you remember about me?

Our apartment—the cats—the old Toyota—and road trip to New Orleans—Sunday breakfast at Morty's—

—And now you're telling me it's all gone, or lost, or put under the heading of "that NPR girl I knew when I was in Madison?" That is so *disappointing*.

I mean—good for you Reed—I'm glad you still have a conscience, or a guilty heart or whatever it is that makes you pay for something that you don't *use* or *enjoy*—

—No, really. I applaud you. I listen to that stuff every day—and I've *never pledged a dime*. They're gonna track me down and kill me, I'm sure—

Why would anyone [pledge]?! you can listen for FREE and THEY DON'T KNOW WHO YOU ARE! Why would you *PAY for that*?

—But the point is: As your ex—as one of your exes—as your former—whatever—lover, girlfriend, partner, soul-mate of twenty-two months—I would just like to think you'd remember something a *little more*...

...*wonderful*. Something with some *ache* in it.

Shooting Star (#3)

Steven Dietz

> Play
> Female
> 40s-50s
> Comic

Upon encountering an old lover at an airport after many years, Elena remembers him fondly. And kind of perversely.

ELENA:

I used to dress him up. Just for fun. He always wore these tan corduroy pants—well, they used to be corduroy, by the time I met him they were thin enough to use as a coffee filter, which we actually did once when we were snowed in and couldn't get to the store.

(…) Anyway…we'd get some cheap red wine in us…and sometimes he'd let me dress him up in some of my dad's old clothes—(…) There was a nice dark suit, a few hand-painted ties, a white shirt that I would clumsily iron. I'd blindfold Reed…dress him in those clothes…put him in front of the mirror…blindfold off…and *voila*! My Own Private Businessman.

He'd adopt poses of "Executives on TV and in Magazines"— pretend to take an urgent call, close a big sale. We'd laugh till our sides hurt—and after about thirty seconds of this…I'd jump him. Throw him on the bed. And, yes, I was—in fact—*stripping my dead father's clothes off my boyfriend and then bedding him with intent.* And yes, I spent plenty of years and thousands of dollars—making sure that dozens of therapists could afford their Volvos and Birkenstocks—all in an effort to deal with the emotional fallout of this, however real or imagined. But, oh my God…Reed McAllister…back then…in that dark suit…man, you would have jumped him, too.

Sometimes Kittens are Your Only Salvation. Cats Can Go Fuck Themselves, Though.

Suzan Hyssen

Blog
Female
35+
Comic

People have a lot of emotions around their felines. Even more so about cute cat videos.

WOMAN:

The other day was so terrible I actually typed the following into my navigation bar:

Cute funny kitten videos

Because it was a bad day. Just stupid bad, where I was crying at my desk, and this was AFTER I had seen my therapist that morning and talked about how much progress I was making with my anxiety and panic.

So. Yeah. I watched a bunch of kittens frolicking like cute, adorable Prozac and I started to feel better. I may also have eaten an enormous piece of dark chocolate, but who hasn't spent a day eating their feelings? You do what you have to to get by.

That evening, when the husband got home from softball, we discussed our days and I told him how I had been just mired in crap and then watched cute kitten videos to feel better.

Husband: ...You realize you have two cats that you don't want anywhere near you.

Me: I know. But they're grown cats and they shed and keep rubbing against me and wanting stuff, and that one shits all over the place. Video kittens are clean and I don't have to clean up their hairballs. Way better.

Husband: ...

Me: Don't even try to understand. (Hold my phone out toward him.) But look at this one! Look how it's dancing!

Husband: ...

Spreadin' the News

Bara Swain

> Play
> Female
> 25-40
> Comic

In her home on the outskirts of Humble, Texas, Mrs. Johnson addresses her 17 year old daughter, Chloe.

MRS. JOHNSON:

(*Animatedly.*) Chloe, this will plum your preserves. Shirlene Carter was decidin' between brown binder rings and teal binder rings for her scrapbooking class, and she saw Martha-Mae Whitfield and her mother buyin' thirty-five imitation eagle feathers over at the Hobby House a week ago Tuesday. Shirlene said them feathers cost more than a wash and a blow-out at the "Curl Up and Dye!" Well, ever'body in Harris County knows that Martha Mae's step-daddy is so tight, his shoes squeak when he walks. And he's an Episcopalian!

So on Wednesday last, Shirlene's mother-in-law treated herself to the early bird special at the Golden Corral in downtown Humble. And while she was peelin' the batter off a her battered Pollock fish fillet on account of her diabetes, she spotted Martha-Mae flirtin' with that chubby busboy whose daddy works the nightshift at the Taco Bell off Kenwick Drive. Anyway, I bumped into Shirlene in the frozen food aisle at the Super K yesterday mornin', and she told me that her mother-in-law told her that Rotary Club President Dwayne Kirby predicts that Martha-Mae and her mother are the top contenders for the five thousand dollar scholarship in the Mother/Daughter Pageant and Dinner Show tonight! (*After a moment.*) Are you listenin' to me?

(*Somberly.*) Oh, their talent is good, Chloe. It's real good. Martha-Mae is performing an interpretive dance inspired by her Comanche ancestors, while her mother recites the *Song of Hiawatha*—in English *and* Spanish!

Chloe, we have to practice if we want a shot at that scholarship money! The talent portion counts for fifty percent of the pageant. That's more than one-third of the overall score!

Spring
Tanya Palmer

> Play
> Female
> Teen
> Comic

Wendy, a young Southern teen, is in front of an assembly, giving a speech. She is wearing a pink dress and white pumps, and holding cue cards.

WENDY:

Okay, everybody, were going to get stared. Umm, hi! Thanks for coming, I'm Wendy Carmichael, for those of you who don't know me.

(Shouts of "Hey Wendy! Wendy!" WENDY giggles.)

And I am running for Queen of Hearts. My first announcement is, whoever threw Mrs. Shobe's chair out of the window during third period yesterday should report to the office before three today if they want to avoid expulsion. That was a very serious offense and somebody could have been killed. Okey dokey. Now I'm going to talk about something serious that's happening right here in our school. Maybe y'all don't know this, but there are people right here, students sitting right beside you, who can't afford to eat lunch, who don't get a decent meal at home, and can't even afford a new pair of shoes let alone a dress for prom. Now maybe some of you are wondering what that has to do with me, Wendy Carmichael. Well, I'll tell you. I'm here cause I want to change all that. I know some of y'all think I'm just a rich girl cause my daddy bought me a new white car this year, and it is really nice. But that could all change tomorrow. Daddy could lose his job and we'd be put on the street pretty quickly. None of us are safe, not even me. I started thinking about what I could do to help those people who are struggling right now to survive. Ms. Handreck suggested we put together an event to help raise money to provide hot meals for students who can't afford to buy their lunch, so that's why I put together this bake sale and silent auction. And If you have any questions about how you can help out, you can come see me at the raffle table.

Stay
David-Matthew Barnes

> Play
> Female
> 17-25
> Comic

Rindy, an aspiring hairstylist who lives in a small Southern town, confides in her best friend Alison that she spent the night with her boyfriend, unbeknownst to her unstable mother. Rindy is extroverted, unfiltered, and Southern.

RINDY:

I pray to God my mother doesn't find out. She hates Tommy. If she knew I was spending the night at his place, she'd probably go mental and kill us all. But, it was worth it. We didn't get much sleep, if you know what I mean. As far as intelligence goes, he was cursed. *(Beat.)* But in other areas…God, I love that man. *(Quick beat.)* I have to stop thinking about him and concentrate on your hair or else Jessie will come home and won't recognize you. He's probably foaming at the mouth just thinking about ripping your clothes off and—sorry. You know how I am. We start talking about boys and I just get carried away. *(Slightly melodramatic.)* My mind starts wandering and I see spots. I get real thirsty, warm, hot. My hands start to shake. All of a sudden, I start to sweat and I get real, real weak. *(Quick beat; unbearable.)* God, I miss Tommy. The son-of-a-bitch doesn't get off work until four o'clock. I'll die before then. I gotta tell you, Ali. You know how I hate it when things get all serious and intense and I have to do something crazy just to make everyone laugh? Well, last night, Tommy looks at me with love and moonlight in his eyes. It was a real movie moment. He says to me, "Rindy, honey, did you enjoy yourself?" So, I rolled over real gently and I stared into his eyes. *(Beat.)* Then, I screamed at the top of my lungs, "Oh my God, Tommy, you have the biggest clock I have ever seen!" His alarm clock. It's huge and it's got these gigantic digital numbers and they're blood red. I swear to you, Alison, I have never seen a clock that big. Not even at Walmart.

That Bitch Brenda Stole My Lip Gloss (and I Want it Back)

David-Matthew Barnes

> Play
> Female
> 17-25
> Comic

> *Brenda Wellington, a glamorous, seventeen-year-old ultimate meangirl, is standing in front of the mirror. With one hand she is applying lip gloss. In the other, she holds her cell phone to her ear. From head to toe, Brenda is dressed to kill.*

BRENDA:

(Into the phone.) Charisma. It's spelled C-H-A-R-I-S-M-A. God, Natasha, don't you know anything? Honestly, I don't think you should be a senior if you can't spell. Maybe I need to go see Principal Grovers and tell him you should still be a junior. He'll hold you back if I ask him to. I might be doing you a favor. Really. Wait. Why are you calling me? Aren't you supposed to be in class? *(Beat.)* I am. I just couldn't stand listening to that woman's awful voice for one more second. She seriously needs to blow her nose. Besides she knows nothing about teaching Spanish. I don't think being a server at Tijuana Charlie's qualifies someone for the job. She won't make it until sixth period. I guarantee it. She already looks like she's been to rehab. Poor thing. She should know better than being a substitute teacher. I mean, we live to terrorize people like her. *(Beat.)* Okay, Natasha, I will tell you. But this is the last time I'm helping you. Seriously, you need to be transferred into remedial classes and spend a weekend picking up trash on the side of the road because you're so stupid. There is no "d" in revenge. R-E-V-E-N-G-E.

This Will Not Look Good on My Resume

Jass Richards

Short story
Female
20s-30s
Comic

Brett talks about the training she received to become a disc jockey, one of a long line of jobs that didn't last very long.

BRETT:

Most people are surprised to hear that deejays are professionally trained. Indeed we are. Not all of us, of course. There are many imposters out there with their rec room stereos and their K-Tel collections. But in order to become a licensed deejay, you have to go through intensive training for two whole weekends.

(…) We were put in groups of four, and each group was assigned a set of equipment that had been sabotaged in some way. One group electrocuted itself. They failed. Another group had a loose connection. Couldn't figure it out. A third group had been supplied with a mono jack instead of a stereo one. So no, it wasn't the speaker. Our group had to build an amplifier with just a piece of string, some bubblegum, a toaster oven, and an instruction manual translated from Japanese. I alone succeeded. Bob, Sam, and Marty refused to read the manual.

During lunch, we had fun with the strobe light and the disco ball. Well, except for Arthur. He had an epileptic seizure. Good to know. For the Epileptic Association's Dinner and Dance.

(…) The last day focused on music styles, tempos, and how to put together a set and how to make generalizations about what kind of music people like based on their age, sex, clothing, and food preferences.

"So you mean my seventy-year-old grandmother can't possibly like Offspring's *Why Don't You Get a Job*?" I asked.

Our trainer, Mr. Music Please, said, "No, she'll like Tommy Dorsey. For her, you would play '*I'll Be Seeing You*'."

I borrowed the guy-next-to-me's cell phone. "Hey Grandma! It's me! Do you like Tommy Dorsey? *I'll Be Seeing You*? Yeah, there's this guy here saying that seventy-year-old grandmothers like Tommy Dorsey. (…) Yeah. I know. All right. I will. Yeah.

Right now? Okay."

(…) She says to tell the asshole she'd rather hear AC/DC.

"Yeah. Love you too, Grandma. Bye." I handed the phone back to the guy-next-to-me.

"Thanks."

Three
Katy Wix

> Freestanding monologue
> Female
> 30s-50s
> Comic

A British woman is just FINE staying home while her friends go out. No, really. Fine. Right as rain.

WOMAN:

No, you go! Don't worry about me! I'll be fine! No, don't worry—you go! Honestly. You go! I'll be absolutely fine.

I was going to stay in anyway and um...paint a table grey. So, yeah. I've been thinking about doing it for a while now so don't worry. Go! Really. Oprah tweeted a picture of herself a few weeks ago painting her table grey and I just connected with the whole grey table vibe immediately. So, don't give it another moment's thought. Go! Go.

Even though it was my idea to go in the first place, that's fine.

Yeah, you have to sand it down a bit first of course, so plenty for me to be getting on with, prep and so on, in fact—stay out! Because there's lots for me to do, so stay out late if you want.

Watch out for that great big puddle just outside—it's been raining quite heavily today—you probably didn't notice -too busy bonding. Too busy staring into each other's eyes. I'm joking of course. (…) Yeah, I sort of feel annoyed, certainly. Mainly because it was my idea originally to go in the first place. But, if there are only two tickets then, well, yes of course you two should go. I mean you've clearly bonded. (…)

So, the headline is: you kids go have fun and I'll stay and hold the fort. It's going to be happy hour here the moment you leave, trust me. (…)

But don't blame me if you come home and I'm slumped over a freshly painted grey table with a cup of bleach in my hand—I'm joking—I wouldn't want to ruin the cup. I'd drink straight from the bottle! But, you go, that's fine. I'll be ok. Maybe I'll paint the walls grey as well and the cups! And the windows and all the tea towels. When you return from your little sojourn everything will be grey... which is really just a metaphor for my life!

The Wedding Plan
Penny Jackson

> Freestanding monologue
> Female
> 23
> Comic

> *Nell "Montana" Sloan, 23, is very attractive Manhattanite, dressed in a cashmere sweater, pearls, and a tweed skirt. She speaks to her wedding planner.*

NELL:

God, I just hate hippies. What's worse—rich hippies. My Mom grew up in Greenwich, Connecticut and went to Miss Porter's School for Girls. That's the place where Jackie O went too. I would have killed to have gone to Miss Porter's School for Girls. But this was the sixties, and my Mom had to get kicked out for—guess what?—smoking dope with the townies. (…)

My childhood was a waste. A hippy dippy trip with too many of my Mom's friends breaking down and sleeping on our couch, in our bathtub, or, once or twice, even sharing my room. (…)

So I think after this little conversation you have a sense of just what kind of wedding I want. No barefoot groom or bride. No vows with quotations from The Sanskrit or Joni Mitchell. I mean, if my wedding were a shirt, it would be so starched that it wouldn't blow away in the wind. If my wedding were a politician, it would be oh…George Bush. Newt Gingrich. Not Obama. You know what I mean. You're a wedding planner. You've done these kinds of weddings before.

Nantucket. Dallas. Charleston. Tuxedoes for the men and bridesmaid dresses that look like they belong on a wedding cake. And guess what? No vegetables. No, my Mom and her friends are going to have to eat dripping red steaks. No smoking either. No pot or even clove cigarettes. Except for cigars. Yeah. Men with Southern accents smoking big fat cigars. That will just make my Mom crazy. Can we do it, please? Please?

Welcome to Christmas Village
Daniel Guyton

> Online magazine post
> Female
> 40+
> Comic

Gingerbell is a female elf. She may be an actual elf, or an actress playing an elf. Either way, she is greeting the audience before a Holiday Show entitled "Welcome to Christmas Village." Maybe Gingerbell should have practiced.

GINGERBELL:

Hello hello! And welcome to Christmas Village! My, what a handsome group you are! *(Her eyes linger on an audience member.)* Yes, very handsome indeed. *(She catches herself.)* Oh! Hahaha! What I mean is! We have a bunch of wonderful surprises in store for you tonight! All certain to get you into the Christmas spirit! Or... Chanukah spirit, if that's what you prefer. We here at the Christmas Village do not discriminate. Not since the lawsuit back in '73. Haha! But anyways, I'm Gingerbell, the Christmas Elf. *(Her eyes linger on him again.)* And I'll be your servant for the evening. Haha! What am I saying? Ok, Let me start over. Hi, my name is Gingerbell, and I'll be your Christmas Elf for the evening! Or... Chanukah elf, I suppose? If... that's what you prefer? *(To that audience member.)* Sir, what cologne are you wearing? Because that's REALLY distracting. No, seriously, I am spraying that all over my pillow tonight. *(Back to the crowd.)* Hahaha! I'm so sorry. This is not like me at all. But in the meantime, here we are at Christmas Village! Aka, Chanukah Village, if that's what you prefer. Where you'll find all sorts of treats and delights aplenty. Oh, I don't even know what I'm saying anymore! *(To the audience member.)* Sir, you are the hottest man I've ever seen. I swear, you look like George Clooney and Burt Reynolds had an illegitimate love child together in the backseat of his Thunderbird. You look like Ryan Gosling all grown up. You look like Matthew McConaughey took a shower! I don't know what you're doing after the show tonight, but I would love to invite you backstage for a tour of Christmas Village. Or... Chanukah Village, if that's what you prefer?

What Corbin Knew
Jeffrey Hatcher

> Play
> Female
> 30s
> Comic

Thada, "bohemian and obnoxious," took on the book club in Crescent Heights, and delights in telling her counterpart, Arno, all about it.

THADA:

So, anyway, I run to the bus so I can cover this book club lunch in Crescent Heights. It's the new trend. Guilt-ridden, middle class women, they read one book a week, then get together to discuss it. This week's book is Henry James' *Portrait of a Lady.* Well, I like Henry James as much as the next person who doesn't enjoy a sentence without a verb. So I get there, and the house is perfect, the hostess is gorgeous, her daughters all have these British names like Prunella and Cressida and Crudite. And then we meet the other "gals," these beautrons with bone structure. (…) Anyway, we sit down for lunch, which is low-fat cottage cheese and iced tea laced with, like, acid and PCPs, and then we go into the library, which my hostess points out has been organized by subject; I sense there's something fishy when I see they've got *Death of a Salesman* in with the murder mysteries. (…) Then we start in on the book, and I'm taking notes when about ten minutes into the discussion, the hostess comes out with the following. "I just didn't think Osmond was handsome." And they all nod and she says, "Yes, Isabel's obsession is understandable in its *context*, but if you'd seen him in that movie where he kept trying to kill Clint Eastwood and the president you just knew he was trouble from the get-go." And I realize…they're talking about John Malkovich. And I know I should keep my mouth shut, but frankly I've had a few Thunderbird Ice Teas myself, and I blurt out; *"You didn't read the book! You're talking about the movie!"* And they stare at me like I've gutted a deer on the rug. (…) I say: "You can't talk about novels you saw at the movies or heard in the car! Besides which, Henry James was not a "Confirmed Bachelor,' he was a closet queen who had his first sexual encounter with the future Chief Justice of the United States Supreme Court, Oliver Wendell Holmes, who set him on the homosexual path for life. Why do you think they called him The Magnificent Yankee? And another thing, *Dorothy*, (…) a book is meant to be READ! You have to look at it. You have to absorb the type face. A work of literature is meant for the eyes!" And the hostess says: "Dorothy is blind."

(Beat.) After that the discussion kid of petered out.

What Scares Me

Suzan Hyssen

Blog
Female
25+
Comic

Sometimes it's the little things. The little, unrecognizable, scary things.

WOMAN:

Sitting on my couch, reading a magazine. I'm not wearing my trifocals, because I can pretty much still read without the print being super fuzzy. It's mostly the distances that fuck me up. I can see that there are photos on the wall across from me, for instance,

BUT I CANNOT MAKE OUT WHAT THE FUCK JUST SKITTERED BEHIND THE PICTURE OF THE PURPLE CHRYSANTHEMUM.

OH HOLY FUCK, WHAT WAS THAT?

I still don't know. I'm sitting here, in my office, hiding. I tried to vacuum up the…thing… but even knocking at the picture with the vacuum extension wouldn't shake anything loose. There is no way in hell I'm going to actually physically touch the picture with my hands, because I know if I get close, I'll end up shaking that… thing…loose on myself.

I hate skittery things.

The cats are useless.

And I'm probably not going to sleep tonight.

Gah.

Of course, it doesn't help that I spent a stupid amount of time on Reddit, reading people's stories of the scariest things they've ever seen. So I sit and wonder, is it a ghost? A Shadow Monster? Is it weird that I HOPE it's a ghost or a Shadow Monster, not because I wouldn't be scared—I totally would shit my pants—but because if it's a ghost or a Shadow Monster, then at least I can have an exorcism or something and then it's over.

If it's a bug, then I don't know where it is and I have to burn the house down and start over.

Oh, my life. It is ridiculous.

UPDATE: The husband came home and I told him about the THING. He mocked me, since I had just recently asked him to kill a spider that turned out to be a tuft of cat hair [I swear, my house is NOT filthy], and then he mocked me some more for not wearing my glasses when I obviously need to [he may have a point there].

So he took the frame off the wall, and looked at the back and didn't see anything, and I thought, "Ok, Shadow Monster—where do I find an exorcist?" and then as he was hanging the frame back on the wall, the MOTHERFUCKING SPIDER SKITTERED BACK OUT. And then he killed it, because he is a man, and that is his purpose.

What the Terrible Psychic Said
Dan Kennedy

> Online magazine post
> Female
> 20+
> Comic

A psychic calls 'em as she sees 'em.

PSYCHIC:

I'm seeing a coastal place, Sausalito, maybe 1977 or 1978. Were you in Fleetwood Mac, or did you own that recording studio where they recorded their second album? No? Do you own a Mac computer? Or maybe a Fleetwood brand luxury motorhome? You probably enjoy sauces, that's what it is, maybe.

Okay, here we go, I'm picking something up here, I'm sensing that you were a…pro motocross racer in a place called Saddleback. Anything? No? Okay, that's okay, have you ever ridden a horse using a saddle, or hurt your back, or enjoyed a company's motto? Or maybe you simply worked in a professional environment at one point. It could be any of those, actually.

You're a playwright and you're single, is that correct? Or maybe you were lonely in a theater recently. It could even be a movie theater. No? Nothing? Okay, that's fine, that's all right. I might just be sensing that you were near a theater once.

Just so you know, this is more difficult than you might think.

Okay, someone is here with me, someone who loves you very dearly and has passed on, she's no longer living, a female presence, maybe a grandmother or your mother? She wants me to tell you something. She says Nipsy Russell likes corn chowder and Taco Bell is owned by monsters. She says whores can see you through your television. No? Nothing?

Okay, you might be blocking the energy. You may not be ready to receive what I'm saying.

Wild with Happy
Colman Domingo

> Play
> Female
> 50s-60s
> Comic

Aunt Glo, an African-American family's matriarch, lectures her nephew, Gil, who wants to scatter family ashes at Disney World.

GLO:

YOU HAVE LOST YOUR MIND! You can't have no funeral services in DISNEY WORLD! I don't know what has been filling your head, excuse my French, LIVING LA VIDA LOCA, but when a person dies, Praise Jesus, there are supposed to be funeral services. A church, a choir, a program, flowers, a casket, help me father, A CASKET! NOT AN URN! What kind of word is that anyway? URNNNNN!!! A wreathe of flowers on the door! You need a wreathe of flowers on the door!!! And a HURST! A HURST!!! Limos for the family with big orange stickers that said funeral on 'em! So other cars know that they shouldn't break the line of cars during the processional. THE PROCESSIONAL!!! What is wrong with you boy? People need a processional! People need to wear black and veils! And WEEP!!! You gotta let people come and weep! FALL OUT and LAY over the casket weep! If they don't weep there, then they could do it at the CEMETERY, where they toss FLOWERS on the CASKET. THE CASKET, not the URN! You don't toss flowers on an URN! Toss flowers on the CASKET AND REACH THEIR GRIEF STRICKEN ARTHRITIC FINGERS TO THE BOWELS OF THE EARTH AS THEIR LOVED ONE IS TAKEN ON AN ELEVATOR TO THEIR FINAL RESTING PLACE SIX FEET UNDER. YOU CAN'T HAVE A FUNERAL SERVICE IN ORLANDO, FLORIDA!!!! YOU CAN'T WEAR BLACK IN FLORIDA!!!

Wine Lovers

Wendy-Marie Martin

> Freestanding monologue
> Female
> 26-40
> Comic

Julia sips her Chardonnay. She loves her Chardonnay. No, really. LOVES it.

JULIA:

Do you realize the power and rich textured complexity you bring to my life?

(Beat.)

The delicious aromas of ripe apple and juicy pear wrapped in warm buttery kisses. The savory scents you echoed on my palate in addition to a squeeze of citrus and an edge of minerality?

(Beat, then to audience.)

What? Never seen a woman talk to her wine before? We're very close. *(Back to wine.)* Aren't we?

(Julia stands, a bit wobbly, and analyzes the crowd.)

Why can't a man be like a good glass of chardonnay, huh? Full-bodied...non- malolactic...you know? They're all so...crisp and refreshing...

Or light and fruity...Where are the meaty flavors? The earth-driven layers...the ones unwilling to sacrifice their innate character? Huh?

(Zeroing in on someone.)

What about you, sweetheart? Feeling jammy and laser-like or angular and austere? Hmmm? I don't like an aggressive aftertaste, you know. Or a blowzy bouquet. You're not...blowzy, are you?

(Really looking at him.)

I'm looking for something course and compact. Expressive and firm. Opulent. You know what I mean? Something...upfront. Toasty. Powerful.

(She flirts with him non-verbally for a bit before realizing it's not going to happen. She stands and straightens herself and returns, head held high, to her seat.)

Bartender? Another Chardonnay, please.

The Women (#1)
Clare Boothe Luce

> Play
> Female
> 34
> Comic

In Luce's classic 1930s commentary on the pampered and powerful, upper middle-class housewife, Sylvia Fowler prowls the bathroom of her younger friend Crystal, who hides behind the shower curtain.

SYLVIA:

Oh, dear, I've lost another pound. I must remember to tell my analyst. You know, everything means something. *(She examines all the bottles and jars on Crystal's dressing table.)* But even my analyst says no woman should try to do as much as I do. He says I attach too much value to my feminine friendships. He says I have a Damon and Pythias complex. I guess I have given too much of myself to other women. He says women are natural enemies — *(Picks up bottle)* Why, Crystal, I thought you didn't touch up your hair — *(Sniffing perfume.)* My dear, I wouldn't use this. You smell it on every tart in New York City. That reminds me — *(Going to shower curtain.)* If you do have an affair, Crystal, for Heaven's sake, be discreet. Remember what Howard did to me, the skunk. *(Peeking in.)* My, you're putting on weight. *(Going back to dressing table.)* But men are so mercenary. They think they own your body and soul, just because they pay the bills — I tried this cream. It brought out pimples—Of course, Crystal, if you were smart, you'd have a baby. It's the only real hold a woman has — Men are so selfish! When you're only making yourself beautiful for them. I wish I could find a man who would understand my need for a companion — !

The Women (#2)

Clare Boothe Luce

> Play
> Female
> 20s-30s
> Comic

In a high-end 1930s New York City salon, Olga, a popular mani-curist dishes while servicing—unbeknownst to her—the betrayed Mrs. Mary Haines.

OLGA:

Know Mrs. Stephen Haines? I guess Mrs. Fowler's told you about her! Mrs. Fowler feels awfully sorry for her. You would if you knew this Crystal Allen. Yes, you know, the girl who's living with Mr. Haines. Oh, I thought you knew. Didn't Mrs. Fowler—? Then you will be interested. You see, Crystal Allen is a friend of mine. She's really a terrible man-trap. She's behind the perfume counter at Saks. So was I before I got fi — left. That's how she met him. It was a couple of month ago. Us girls weren't busy. It was an awful rainy day, I remember. So, this gentleman walks up to the counter. He was the serious type, nice-looking, but kind of thin on top. Well, Crystal nabs him. "I want some perfume," he says. "My I awsk what type of women for?" Crystal says, very ritzy. That didn't mean a thing. She was going to sell him our feature, Summer Rain, anyway. "Is she young?" Crystal says. "No," he says, sort of embarrassed. "Is she the glamorous type?" Crystal says. "No, thank God," he says. "Thank God?" Crystal says, and bats her eyes. She's got those eyes which run up and down a man like a searchlight. Well, she puts perfume on her palm and in the crook of her arm for him to smell. So he got to smelling around, and I guess he liked it. Because we heard him tell her his name, which one of the girls recognized from Igor Cassini's column — Gee, you're nervous — Well, it was after that I left. I wouldn't of thought no more about it. But a couple of weeks ago I stopped by where Crystal lives to say hello. And the landlady says she'd moved to the kind of house where she could entertain her gentleman friend — "What gentleman friend?" I says. "Why, that Mr. Haines that she'd had up in her room all hours of the night," the landlady says — *(Mary draws back her hand.)* Did I hurt?

The Worst Production of The Snow Queen Ever
Kemuel DeMoville

> Play
> Female
> 30+
> Comic

Eloise stand in front of the curtain and welcomes everyone to, well...see the title.

ELOISE:

Hello! Hello everyone! Oh I'm so glad you all came. Hello, hello there in the back row. Yes I can see you! Hello, hello, hello. Well you all look really excited to be here, especially you. Look at you, you look like you're about ready to pounce out of your seat. Just like a little leopard, pounce, pounce, pounce! Welcome all of you to the first ever semi-annual bi-yearly twice-daily fundraiser for the preservation of obscure Danish Fairytales. Actually, here's an added bonus, the Danish government has agreed to offer a tax write-off to any citizen of Denmark who attends this performance. So if any of you are Danish people be sure to save your ticket stubs. The only Danish person I know is my Aunt Bethel...she eats three bearclaws every day! Get it? Danish...Bearclaws...yes, yes, I'm sure you get it. My jokes are like the flu, you don't want it, but you get it. Well I guess we should get down to business. My name is Eloise Perkins and I am assistant treasurer for the Social Organization for the Preservation and Furthering of Social Awareness toward Provincial Folk and Fairy Tales. Incidentally, for any of you who wish to make a donation to our organization you don't have to write out that long name on the check. Just use our clever Acronym, SOPFSAPFFT. That's S-O-P-F-S-A-P-Double F-T. Simple! Now I've been asked to come out here and sort of introduce the show, warm the audience up and all that. I guess I am the one person here who has the longest background in theatre, you see I come from a somewhat famous theatrical family, much like the Lunts or Barrymores. I actually have a brother, who's gone quite far in the business. It started with a couple of guest spots on "America's Most Wanted," which led to a segment on "Cops," and right now he's starring in a documentary for HBO entitled "Behind the Bars:

An Inmate's Journey to Self-discovery." So for those of you with cable be sure to set your VCR's. I guess I should say a little about the production that you are here to see. As I have already mentioned this is a fundraiser for our organization, so what we have tried to do tonight is make this experience enjoyable for everyone. We put the "Fun" in "Fundraise." Tonight's performance will be an adaptation of a little known Fairytale entitled "The Snow Queen." Some of you may have heard of it, if so um…kudos!

(Salutes)

Literacy, I salute you! Just don't spoil the ending for anyone who's not quite as studious as you are.

Male
Comic Monologues

7th Period Lunch, or Someone's Gonna Snap (#1)
David Don Miller

> Play
> Male
> 41
> Comic

Mr. Moe Puglese, a big bully who passes for a high school assistant principal, clicks on the school intercom to make announcements prior to state testing. He is prone to Italian idioms, malapropisms, and impropriety.

MR. PUGLESE:

Attention students. As we are in the midst of testing, we wanna nip some issues in the butt. That means all of your electronicals need to be removed from your person prior to entering the demarcalated testing areas. If you are caught with an electronical in the testing areas, your test will be invalidated, irregardless of the reason for the presence of your electronical. So take it out now so we can bag it, tag it, book it, and cook it. Or…hide it and hope for the best. But if it goes off in the testing room? Your entire test, everything you worked for, all that effort goes bye-bye, capice? And while I'm at it, I know it's getting hot out…and summa you girls like to dress like you're hangin' out at the beach. And I'm not sayin' the boys don't appreciate it, 'cause believe me, we do—*they do*. But be that as it may be, we are trying to create a maximum optimum testing environment. So that means if you're wearing a belly shirt, a spaghetti strapped blouse, you got some shorts climbin' up in your—*(Whistles "woo-hoo")*—or, if you got a thong and a skirt that barely covers you know what…you're gonnahafta, you know, come down to my office and kindly remove those clothing items. Thank you and good luck.

10 Ways to Survive the Zombie Apocalypse
Don Zolidis

> Play
> Male
> 20s
> Comic

Sam is giving an inspirational speech to a few survivors of the zombie apocalypse.

SAM:

Now listen up troops. We've only got a few minutes before the zombies cross that ridge so it's time for me to give an inspirational speech. (…)

Go ahead and sit. Sit for yourself. Sit for this country. Sit for humanity. I want you to sit for everyone you've ever loved, the girl you loved desperately and never found the courage to talk to.

Now you might think to yourself: What can I do, one person, against an army of unstoppable zombies? We've seen them. We know how many there are. A lot. I mean, so many zombies that they can literally walk over each other to climb up skyscrapers. I don't need to tell you that that's a lot of zombies. And yes, we're likely to die horribly and then rise from the dead and join them in a tidal wave of nightmarish destruction that will sweep over the planet. That's a likely scenario. Hopefully we won't feel too much pain. Probably will. Probably be excruciating. You know when you go the dentist? This is going to be a lot worse than that. This is going to be like a million dentists poking you at the same time. I know what you're thinking: How will all those dentists even reach me? But let's say they're tiny dentists. But their needles still hurt as much as regular-sized needles. That's probably in the same range of the amount of pain we're likely to feel when the zombies tear us limb from limb.

What was I talking about again?

After (#2)
Chad Beckim

> Play
> Male
> Early 30s
> Comic

Warren, an Indian man, works in a doggy day-care center where Monty seeks employment. He gives Monty the lowdown.

WARREN:

I thought I loved dogs, too. I really did. I would see them on the street or in the park, and I would pet them and talk to them. But then I started working with them. And now I'm not so sure. Actually, I can't stand most of them. Little fuckers.

We chauffeur dogs here. I can't get over that. I understand the brushing and washing and feeding and all that. But chauffeuring? Like they're kids coming home from a field trip?

Our priorities are so screwed up. When you think about it, people are out there starving and these dogs are eating three course meals. You see the homeless guys outside sometimes, watching the dogs eat. One lady brings her dog to a pet therapist. What the hell does a dog need a therapist for? They eat, sleep, shit and fight. The shit people will waste their good money on. Let's face it, it's a fucking dog, dude. Chinese people eat dogs. Did you know that?

When I was a kid we had a yellow lab. Lived outside. Ate dry food—and take it from me? Avoid that wet stuff, dude. That wet stuff makes them shit pudding. But my dog. Didn't even need to be chained up. Came and went as he pleased. And he seemed perfectly happy–lived until he was 13, I think…got rabies when he protected my mother from a wolf. So my father made me put him down myself. *(He cocks his finger like a gun.)* Pow! It was sad.

I was just joshing. I never had a dog. Anyway, this is really not a bad place to work. *(A loud yapping of a dog fight comes through the door.)* Abigal! Cut the shit, right now! Don't get tough with me, Miss Thing! I'll put your ass in time out! You know the drill.

She's a nasty bitch, though. And the way she looks at me. Sometimes I half expect her to talk back to me.

Do you play chess?

Bobby Wilson Can Eat His Own Face
Don Zolidis

> Play
> Male
> 40s
> Comic

Coach Borney, a military man masquerading as a gym teacher,
torments Bobby, a freshman in high school.

COACH:

Look at these stringy little arms! You call yourself a man?! (…)
You're not eighteen! Hey boys! We got a little baby over here!
How 'bout we put you back in the nursery—is it naptime for little
baby? You disgust me, Wilson! You're nothing but a worm! A
little, tiny, insignificant worm! Hey, does anyone here besides me
want to punch Wilson in the face? I've got some advice for you,
Wilson. You know how you get ahead in life? By being meaner
and stronger than the guy next to you. You gotta push their faces in
the mud if you're ever gonna walk. So what I'm telling you to do
is every day after school, you better be in that weight room there
lifting, getting stronger, getting bigger—start out with something
small, that you can handle, like peas, and then from peas you can
move up to marshmallows, and if you work at it real hard you can
start lifting oranges. You understand? (…)

There are certain laws in society, Wilson. We have laws out
there and then we have laws in here. And the law in here is this:
when I say side-straddle hops, you bring your hands all the way
together on the upswing making a CLAPPING sound! If you do not
make that sound, it is not a correct side-straddle hop. OBSERVE.

(COACH BORNEY counts and does four perfect jumping jacks.)

ONE two three four TWO two three four THREE two three
four FOUR two three four. HUP!

That is how a man performs side-straddle hops. That is how
a man who killed three Viet Cong with his bare hands does side-
straddle hops. If you ever want to kill a man with your bare hands,
you'd better learn to do a side-straddle hop. Understand?

Changelings (#1)
Reina Hardy

> Play
> Male
> 26-40
> Comic

Magus Kemp lectures his introductory magic class, held in secret at the University of Chicago.

MAGUS:

Magic.

Practical magic. Applied magic. Real magic. If you are sitting in this classroom, you are in a select cadre of mildly talented and exorbitantly obsessed people who know, deep in their hearts, that such a thing exists. Freaks.

I am Magus Kemp, ThD. Magus, not Professor, thank you. I am a board-certified Walker to the seventh level, capable of at-will travel between eleven separate dimensions, and the only such person extant in the United States. If you remain in any doubt as to my credentials, if you are thinking, "This man is a crank, and unstable," you are correct. I am mildly insane.

If any of you have ever dabbled in drugs, and I can state with ninety percent accuracy that you all have, it's as if I'm on a quarter tab of mescaline at all times.

Welcome!

First axiom. Magic is almost, but not entirely, completely gone from this world. Second axiom. Chicago is the only remaining center of magical studies on all continents. Not Europe, not Africa, here. There are two reasons why you have come, from all across the globe, from older and more mysterious places than the United States, to study magic. The first is the fine thaumaturgical library maintained by the University of Chicago, founded with the acquisition of the Sorbonne's entire stock on the subject after a series of unpleasant incidents at the 1893 World's Fair. A century long program of aggressive purchase and theft...mostly theft...has left us with a collection generally agreed to be the best in the world.

This is referred to as academic magic, and it is bunk. Complete and utter horseshit.

Changelings (#2)

Reina Hardy

> Play
> Male
> 26-40
> Comic

Magus Kemp warns his introductory magic class (held in secret at the University of Chicago) about a new supernatural danger.

MAGUS:

Greetings, class. Many apologies for my slight, entirely understandable tardiness. I have come here today at great peril. This room is dangerous—this concentration of enchanted minds is like tinder in a lighting storm. I would not be here at all, had I not come down with a sudden fit of qualms. You are a pallid, cloying lot, but as it turns out I would rather you did not all die.

Please remain calm, and digest this litany of facts.

Last night, at 1:46 am, an unexpected thaumic shockwave caused all fireflies and cicadas within a three-mile radius of Hyde Park to spontaneously combust. This morning, all area statues depicting female persons or feline animals were found to be in altered positions, their faces fixed in expressions of rage. On Oakley Road, a grapevine broke down a door and strangled someone's dog.

Don't you see what this means? Run! Go! Scatter yourselves like rice! There is something loose in the world that must not be spoken of—forget all you learned here. Forget all you can. Put yourself into a coma if you can afford it.

For the love of god, class dismissed!

Check Please: Take 3

Jonathan Rand

> Play
> Male
> 20s
> Comic

Barry is on a first date. Chances of a second date? You decide.

BARRY:

Shall we get started?

I recently underwent a failed merger with my previous client. What I'm looking for at this stage is a floor-to-ceiling overhaul of the status-quo—a paradigm shift that will take us to the next level—bring us from a relationship...to Relationship 2.0. (...)

Please hold your questions till the end. (...) My four-year plan is to hit the ground running with a strong foundation in the first three quarters, synergizing from the word Go, and fully reinvent our relationship using a game-changing, scalable approach to seamless integration.

How exactly do I *plan* to accomplish this? I'll tell you:

Thinking outside-the-box.

Win-win situations.

Giving 110 percent.

Maximizing leverage.

Pushing the envelope.

Squaring the circle.

And finally...making sure we call ahead if one of us is going to be late for a movie or something.

I think you'll agree that as a disruptive innovation, this is a value-added proposition. If we run it up the flagpole and see who salutes; if we skate to where the puck is going; if we stick a fork in it to see if it's done; if we tickle the artichoke till it sings "Dancing Queen"—then I guarantee this merger will bear fruit.

And by "bear fruit" I am in no way referring to babies.

Unless you want to talk about it.

But totally cool if not.

I want four.

(Beat.)

Any questions?

Christopher Hiney
Roy Proctor

> Play
> Male
> 20s
> Comic

Christopher Hiney surveys the contents of the pool at an exclusive retirement community. He wears a rainbow-striped Speedo and a whistle lanyard. He carries a clipboard and a cell phone is clipped to his Speedo.

CHRISTOPHER:

Welcome to the new pool at the Garden of Earthly Delights, our fair city's first retirement community for old gays and lesbians. I'm Christopher Hiney, your water-exercise instructor. Here are the rules of the pool: No diving, no cannon-balling, no goosing, no groping, no grabbing, no flashing. Any questions? (…)

Yes, Mr. Denny, I'm gay, gloriously gay. I live in a double-wide mobile home with my boyfriend, Bruce, the love of my life. *(Blows whistle.)* Now listen up. In this class, we'll be following the Fabulous Water Sports Regimen by Christopher, which I'm—*(Ringtone sounds: puts phone to ear.)* What now?…I'm teaching, damn it… Go to hell, Bruce, and take your goddam stuff with you. Last night was the last straw, you slut. BYE!…

Sorry, gentlemen. Any more questions? (…) Yes, you heard right. Once a year, we'll put on an Aquacade show. Glitzy-glitz! Hurray for the Golden Age of Hollywood!

(Ringtone; jerks phone from Speedos.) Dammit, Bruce!… You're bugging the hell—Are you out of your fucking mind?… No, you MAY NOT move in with my mother…I don't give a shit how much she likes you. She doesn't know what a goddam slut you are. SLUT! HUSSY! STRUMPET! Bye! *(Rams phone down into crotch.)*

Sorry about that, gentlemen. Any more questions? (…) No, Mr. Gibbs, you may NOT pee in the pool. Go pee in your bathtub… Well, pee in your shower, then…

(Nervously.) Just where do you think you're going, Mr. Gibbs?…Mr. Mallory? You're up to no good. I know it. You're

going to pee in the shower together. *(Ringtone; slams phone against his ear.)* What is it, Mama?…No, Bruce CANNOT move in with you. *(Covers phone.)* Mr. Smith. Come back. Please!…Mama, if you dare, I'll never speak to you again. *(Covers phone.)* Mr. Poindexter. Where are you going? Mr. Earnhardt? Mr….What's happening here?…Bye, Mama!..I love you, too. *(Returns phone to Speedo.)*

No, this class is not a waste of time. It's the fulfillment of your dreams! Please come back. You don't know what you're doing. Oh, shit!

(Turning on '50s rock 'n' roll on his phone, begins to exercise, shouting over the music.) Jumping Jacks, gentlemen. Watch me. Legs as wide as you can. Coordinate, gentlemen, coordinate! Arms, legs, arms, legs…Back straight, head up…Great, gentlemen!

Consider the Oyster

David MacGregor

> Play
> Male
> 20s
> Comic

Eliot helps a friend who is transitioning to a female to own it—right down to the shoes.

ELIOT:

Gene, you're a male, female, straight, gay, transgender mother lode of discrimination possibilities. You're every attorney's wet dream. But you still can't show up at your school and go stomping around like a Neanderthal. Now slip those heels on and let's see how you look. Okay...now, let's see you walk. There we go! Glide...glide...chin up, come on...get those shoulders back a little... steady...eyes on the horizon. Remember, you're a fabulous babe, that means you don't make eye contact with anyone...come on, put some life into it...you're not gliding. Okay, stop.

You're not getting this. Men and women walk differently, all right? Get that through your head. Walking is all about context... who you're with, what you're doing, and so on. You've got your regular walk, right? But if you're a man, and you're on the prowl, out comes the chest, little bit of a strut, "Here I am, world! I'm big, I'm bad, and I take what I want! Now outta my way, or I'll mow you down!" But if you're a woman, it's a completely different walk. You get that hip twitch going, get your junk moving side to side like it's nobody's business. "That's right. I got it. You want it. You get hold of this caboose and I'll take you for the ride of your life." You see what I mean?

The Craft (#1)
Andrew Biss

Play
Male
20s-30s
Comic

The Actor has a cocky, bravura exterior that masks the frustrated, insecure actor within. As he steps onto the stage in character, we are privy to his inner dialogue.

ACTOR:

Act Two, Scene Three. I enter from stage right...nervous but in character, cross to the chair placed downstage center, next to the small table, and sit. I look up, seemingly forlorn, and begin my brief soliloquy that speaks of the turmoil and heartache inside of me that was all-too-obviously telegraphed in the previous scene.

(Beat.)

I direct it to the fourth wall, as if speaking to anyone and no one, *and yet*...some woman in the third or fourth row is wearing a blouse of a color so loud and garish that I find my peripheral vision is being constantly distracted by it, thus diminishing the gravitas of what I'm attempting to impart to the audience at large. God I hate her – she's really screwing this up for me.

(Beat.)

I'm ignoring her as best I can and concentrate on the words. Okay, I'm done. God, I hate her – she really threw me off.

(Beat.)

I think my expression at the end really got them, though... despite the distraction of Coco the Clown in row C or D or wherever the hell she is.

(Beat.)

All right then, darling, let's be having you...make your entrance please...*now.*

(Beat.)

Christ, where is she? Come on, come on!

(Beat.)

All right, don't panic. Try to look deep in thought, as if there's a very important inner dialogue raging inside of you – then maybe the audience will think it's all deliberate.

(Beat.)
God, I could strangle her right now! *Where the hell is she?*

The Craft (#2)
Andrew Biss

Play
Male
20s-30s
Comic

The Actor has a cocky exterior that masks the insecure actor within. As he waits for his scene partner to finish her monologue, he shares his inner monologue.

ACTOR:

I wonder if there's any agents in the audience tonight. I invited six but none of them responded. Wait a second…that guy back there with the glasses looks like he might be.

(Beat.)

On second thoughts, no…too hip. Useless bastards. I expect they were all "too busy". Yeah, too busy propping up some bar, getting wasted after a hard day's skimming cash off the backs of their client's hard work. Parasites. They should be sat out there doing their job…scouting for talent…witnessing art.

(Beat.)

Oh, look out—her big speech is about to end. And not before time. She milks that thing like a Jersey cow.

(Beat.)

And if there are any agents out there tonight, I hope they're taking note, because *this* is acting. Not only am I having to navigate this scene alone with Ling-Ling here, but I mean, really—he had an abortion two years ago after a brief romp in the rhododendrons with the former gardener? I mean, who writes this crap? I'm supposed to be shocked and appalled by this revelation? It's hardly the stuff of Gran Guignol. Now, if she'd been raped by her father and given birth to a hideously deformed, inbred monstrosity that she kept chained to a post behind the summerhouse, *then…then* we'd have a revelation…*then* we'd have something to work with. But no, it's just your average, plain vanilla abortion saga, in response to which—and to great effect, using every skill at my disposal—I fix her with a steely gaze that betrays neither outrage nor compassion.

Ziegler & Capecci

Dad, Can I Please Get Machine Gun Your Face 4 For Christmas?

Stephen Statler

Online magazine post
Male
9-13
Comic

A boy makes a compelling Christmas wish.

BOY:

Dad, can I please get *Machine Gun Your Face 4* for the Xbox? Logan has it and Caden has it. It's way less violent than *Machine Gun Your Face 3*. The blood is like purple, it's not even realistic, and the things you kill are like aliens, they're not even real people. And you can't shoot bystanders, I know, because I played the demo at Evan's. Evan actually has *Bystander 3*, where all you do is shoot bystanders, and I don't even like that one. It's too violent.

Plants vs. Zombies is boring! None of my friends play it because it's so boring. And *Machine Gun Your Face* is not even rated "Mature," it's rated "Teen." Logan isn't even eight and his dad lets him play *Kill Everything 2*, which is way more bloody than *Machine Gun Your Face* and *Kill Everything 1*.

You don't know anything about *Machine Gun Your Face* because you only saw the trailer. Noah's dad plays *Strafer 4* all day on his couch, and he lets Noah play *Jugular Cutter 2*, where all you do is slit the guy's throat and the blood is real. Noah and I can't even play when I'm there because his dad's always playing. And he's really good, he's like the best in the country. He also lets Noah play *Jugular Cutter 2* before he goes to bed. And Noah doesn't even have bad dreams.

I don't want to play basketball, it's so boring! All you do is shoot and shoot and then Tyler just kicks the ball into the street, and you don't even let me go get it. So it takes like an hour to play one game. And Mom makes me put on sunscreen when it's like five in the afternoon, and Tyler's mom brings out pears and stands there till we eat them all. Just get me *Machine Gun Your Face 4* and I swear I won't ask for anything else for Christmas. Except for *Bleedout 6*, which is way less violent than *Bleedout 5*. The blood isn't even real.

Dating After 50 (#1)

Terence Duncan

> Freestanding monologue
> Male
> 50+
> Comic

Dating after 50. You've been there. If you haven't, you will. Or maybe you won't. But if you do, be afraid.

TERRY:

The most important thing I can share with you is that I am a reluctant dater.

Being over 50, dating is pure drudgery. When I was young and dating, it was all so much fun—like one big adventure, with the thrill of conquest and passion…going to see cool movies, holding hands, talking on the phone for hours… And, if I thought it would get me laid, I'd even dance. It took a lot of energy, but I had a lot of energy. I didn't need to sleep. My priorities were getting my degree, partying and getting laid—in that order. Now? Now my priorities are sleep, work, and…food. Sure, I still think about getting laid, but only to the extent that it doesn't interfere with my first three priorities— especially sleep. The problem is, dating always seems to interfere with sleep. Back when I was young, a date wouldn't even start until 10:00, and we'd stay up 'till four in the morning! Not now. Now, I like to set up a 6:00 dinner date, so if things don't go well, I can still be home in time to watch *Myth Busters* and be asleep by 10:00.

Even the basic purpose of dating has changed for me. Dating used to be all about sex—or the possibility of sex. Now? Now it's little more than an affirmation that someone would still want to go out and have dinner with me. It's an ego thing. I don't really want to date. I just want to know that I *can* date. After all, you go out…you have dinner…but, once you eat…what happens? You get tired and want to take a nap. The worst thing a woman can say to me after dinner is, "Now what do you want to do?" What do you mean, what do I want to do? I'm done! The date is over. I want to go home and go to sleep. That's what I want to do. Unless of course, you want to have sex, but even then, I'm only gonna give you a half hour and I'm not taking you to my place, 'cause it's a mess.

Dating After 50 (#2)
Terence Duncan

> Freestanding monologue
> Male
> 50+
> Comic

Terry gets a roadie.

TERRY:

The first woman I went out with—while my divorce was pending, wasn't good at dating either, and I thought that might be a good thing. But, I couldn't tell if she liked *me* or if she just liked the idea of me, or anyone who'd pay attention to her and get her family off her back for not having a boyfriend. Seriously, I felt like any ol' guy in the tux on the cake. We went out once and all of a sudden we're "dating." Can't a guy tell a woman he loves her without it turning into a commitment?! She kept calling me "honey." She called me all the time— TO TALK! TO HANG OUT! "What are you up to?" Argh! "Why don't you come over. We can hang out." I don't want to hang out! It's 7:00! I've already taken my pants off. Can't we just get together on the weekends? "You should take the day off and come over". To do what??? Talk? I can't just call in sick. I have a Power Point Presentation to pull together!! And, you know, to this day, I'm still mad at her. I'm trying to remember her name. I think it was Kathy or Janet or something.

The first time we went out, I picked her up at her place. She was like, 35 or 45, and I think she was going back to school or starting a new job or something…to study…nursing or English or something—or maybe she already had a job. I don't remember. I do remember she had on a pleated, plaid skirt and black leotards, with a red sweater…very sexy. Anyway, I went to her house and we chatted for a while. We were gonna go to a movie. Before we left she asked me if I wanted a 'roadie." I had never heard that term before, but I assumed it was…you know…a blow-job. Well, she goes to the kitchen and comes back with two beers— to drink in the car. That's what a Roadie is. Drinking in the car! That's illegal! So, not only am I disappointed that I'm not getting a blow job, but she wants to turn me into a felon! I know I could have avoided the frustration had I just asked, "If by 'roadie', you mean blow-job, then yes. Yes I would." In fact, I should do that all the time. If by "coffee" you mean blow-job, then yes. If by "Do you want your receipt?" you mean "Do you want a blow job," then, yes I would. That was it for her. You should never tease a guy about blow-jobs.

Dating After 50 (#3)
Terence Duncan

Freestanding monologue
Male
50+
Comic

Who was it who said, "Know thyself?" Oh, right: this guy.

TERRY:

I love dating alcoholics. They really don't care if you listen to them and you can talk them into anything. O.K., it's not so much talking them into things, it's more like not waking them up. But, let's face it, if it weren't for alcohol, no one over fifty would ever have sex. None of us look like we did in our 20s and thirties. Hell, I had a twenty-nine-inch waist. Twenty-nine inches!!! I'm pretty sure my thighs are bigger than that now. How is a sober woman supposed to get excited about that? If I can be honest with you I hardly recognize some of the female body parts any more. After fifty, no one should attempt naked sex. Trust me, leave your clothes on. You just have to make sure there are strategically placed zippers that provide the minimum access. I've even had Velcro surgically stitched to my back, so it's impossible to pull my t-shirt off. Thank God for alcohol.

The problem is, not *all* women are alcoholics. Waaaay too many of them are *recovering* alcoholics. They don't drink ANY MORE! What the hell??!! What is even the point of going out if they're not going to drink? Even if sex isn't on the table, at my age, nobody cares what anybody else thinks about anything. We all have our four or five good stories to tell (over and over) and that's how we communicate. We just wait for the other person to stop talking about herself so we can talk about ourselves. That's why being an alcoholic is a virtue. Being a recovering alcoholic is just a form of baggage and by the time you're fifty, you are carrying *too much baggage anyway.* That dog you love so much? Baggage. Your intolerant political beliefs? Baggage. Your unwillingness to perform a good roadie? B A G G A G E ! It's best to find someone whose baggage doesn't clash with yours. For instance, You're OCD? Great! Find a hoarder who likes to be told what to do. Are you drowning in credit card debt? That's O.K. Find a co-dependent workaholic with a savior complex. You have the ex from hell? Great. Find a serial killer!

Dating After 50 (#4)

Terence Duncan

> Freestanding monologue
> Male
> 50+
> Comic

"Marriage is like being a frog in boiling water...you slowly get used to it."

TERRY:

It's nearly impossible to maintain positive self-esteem when you're dating in your fifties. I was in a hotel recently and the bathroom door had a mirror on it. So, as I'm sitting on the toilet, I get to look at myself...sitting on the toilet—full frontal view, with my underwear around my ankles—big belly bulging out, bed hair raging. That's not me!!! That's not the image I have of myself!! I'm the guy who wears ties and goes on business trips. I'm the guy in the Dos Equis ad who doesn't always drink beer. The mirror was right in front of the toilet! What sadistic underwear model designs a bathroom like that?

I think it's even harder for women. They have to deal with the whole change of life thing. I've had more than one woman tell me about how they feel like they've lost their value to society once they can't have children. About how men don't hold the door open for them anymore, or won't buy them drinks, and how they can't smile their way out of traffic tickets. They seem to go out of their way to convince you how unattractive they are. Again, think of the pressure this puts on the guy trying to date them. Somehow, you've got to get them feeling good enough about themselves to want to have sex with you. "Listen, I know you're not as attractive as you once were. But, I'm willing to drink enough to look past that. The least you can do is drink enough not to care."

Actually, I think that's the value in staying married into old age. When you've loved someone a long time, you're having sex with how attractive the person used to be. You hold onto that, because you love them. It's kind of like the frog in the boiling water; you're used to each other. When you're divorced, you have nothing but the here and now. That's why I'm so damn bitter. That's why I don't like dating, and that's why I'm gonna go to bed as soon as I get home, which won't be fast enough. That is, of course, unless one of you single ladies has had too much to drink.

Dialogues of the Dead (#1)

Lucian, adapted by Baudelaire Jones

Play
Male
60+
Comic

Mr. Bass brags about his young lovers, and the maid who won, if not his heart, then certainly his fortune.

MR. BASS:

You missed out, Mr. Bean—the golden years were really something! I could do what I liked—there were still plenty of beautiful women and fine bottles of wine to enjoy. I became known for my extravagant parties. Oh, I never paid a penny out of my own pocket. All of these things were gifts, you see, from my many admirers. Only the cream of the crop was allowed in my presence! The best society had to offer! The brightest and most beautiful! Young gods and goddesses—all eager to please! They had eyes only for me! I was just as you see me now—old, bald, bleary-eyed, arthritic ... and the object of all desire. I had to beat them off with a stick. I should have thought you knew the violent passion for old men who have plenty of money and no children. But I assure you, Mr. Bean, I nevertheless took a great deal of satisfaction in my young lovers. They idolized me. Showered me with gifts. Threw parties. I had an almost godlike power over them. They couldn't refuse me anything—a discovery that came in particularly handy with the ladies. Sometimes I would play games—cut some of them off. Such rivalries! You wouldn't believe! Such jealous competition! I promised to make each of them my sole heir—and they believed me! Every one of them! The little piggies! If they'd ever had an honest conversation with each other, they would have figured it out—but they didn't! They just pranced around, secretly laughing at the others—secure in the knowledge that they would win out in the end! Of course, my actual will told them all to go hang. The actual beneficiary was my maid. Beautiful girl. About twenty. I'm sure you can guess her job description! Well, I'll say this—she deserved the money more than they did. She didn't love me either, of course—but she was honest about the whole thing. She didn't put on airs like the rest of them. And they all treated her like dirt. Now they can kiss her ass!

Dialogues of the Dead (#2)
Lucian, adapted by Baudelaire Jones

Play
Male
30s
Comic

Lord Dinwitty tells a tale of intrigue, woe, and irony.

LORD DINWITTY:

You remember Lord Carlsbad? Lonely old bugger. Lots of money. No children. Well, I'd spoken kindly to him on occasion—even took him out to dinner once or twice. He was so grateful that one day, quite out of the blue, he promised to make me his sole heir. His sole heir! He's worth millions, you understand! I couldn't believe my luck. I hadn't asked for it—never thought of it, really—but from that day forward, in order to show my appreciation, you know, I began to spend practically every waking moment in his company. I'd drop by first thing in the morning. We'd play checkers. Shuffleboard. At first, it wasn't so bad—not terribly exciting, but I'd just think of the money, and that would keep me going. After a few weeks, though, I began to run out of steam. He liked to tell war stories—never actually fought in the war, mind you—spent most of the war typing in some office in Liverpool. Try to imagine, if you will, war stories that involve mostly typing—an occasional flirtation with the frumpy secretary or a heated debate over the proper use of the semicolon. It was interminable! I knew I couldn't keep it up much longer. Still, the inheritance! I couldn't stop thinking about it! I'd already spent most of it in my head! I began thinking up ways to hurry him along, if you know what I mean. Little things, at first. I convinced him to take up cricket—thought the exertion might be too much for his heart. But it only made him healthier! Suddenly he looked ten years younger! I took him boating—thought he might fall in and drown—I even went so far as to rock the boat a little. But the old bugger had impeccable balance, and, worse luck, he always wore a lifejacket. I began to get desperate. Finally, I decided to approach the butler. He was an unhappy little man—bitter that he had himself been overlooked for the inheritance. Together, we concocted a plan. Are you familiar with ricin? No? It's a powerful poison—extracted from castor beans, of all things—twice as deadly as cobra venom! The butler agreed to administer the poison the next time his master called for wine—which he did constantly. He was a drunken sot. In return, I promised to reward the poor fellow for all his years of loyal service—something his master had never done. The next evening, after our usual activities, the servant brought two cups—the poisoned one for Carlsbad—and the other for me. Unfortunately, the incompetent oaf got nervous, switched the cups somehow—gave me the poisoned cup, and a few minutes later, much to my surprise, there I was—dead on the floor and cheated out of my inheritance. *[LORD MARLBOROUGH laughs.]* I suppose you think it's very funny. So did the old man. After he got over the initial shock, he put it all together, I guess, and laughed hysterically at his butler's mistake.

Don't Call Us, We'll Call You
Abigail Taylor Sansom

> Play
> Male
> 26-40
> Comic

Is Cal a brilliant writer-director-auteur...or is he making this shit up?

CAL:

You've got a lot of range, you know. When I called you in for *Care Bears LIVE!*, I was thinking of you more as a potential Cheer Bear or Funshine Bear, but you just tore those walls down. Now I'd even consider Tenderheart Bear or Grumpy Bear. Maybe even the Cloud Keeper—if we decide to cast non-traditionally, of course. Just F.Y.I., we're currently in the process of rewrites. Our playwright, David Mamet, is very particular. He only likes to show the finished product...

What?

Oh. Pseudonym. He's got an ego, but he needs the paycheck. Writers. Um... Well...

It all starts in the Kingdom of Caring. And you've got all these Care Bears and shit. And they're like caring and sharing, and all that. And then, all of a sudden, bam! Good Luck Bear gets super sick. And he keeps asking for Rosebud, but nobody knows what Rosebud is. So they leave the Forest of Feelings and go to a galaxy far, far away, where they meet Professor Coldheart. But little do they know, he's actually Friend Bear's true biological father. Then they come to Earth and they all create a bobsled team—even though everyone laughs at them because the Forest of Feelings is very warm and therefore unsuitable for bobsledding. But they go on to the Olympics and kick some ass anyway. Then they return to Castle Care-a-lot, where they realize that Rosebud was Good Luck Bear's sled. And that's the show. Kind of existentialist, isn't it? I'm a big fan of Brecht.

The Enigma Variations
Evan Guilford-Blake

> Play
> Male
> 20s
> Comic

In the parlor of an English country home in 1920, Richard breathlessly addresses Isobel's father.

RICHARD:

You see, sir, Isobel's so—marvellous; so wonderfully—marvellous. Just like her mother. And I do love her so. Isobel. Of course. I know she's still quite young, and so am I, but, well—it's not un*heard* of, and I've known of several couples of our ages who've been quite successful.

(In one breath.)

I'm doing quite well at University, sir, I'm certain to finish in another year, and my father's arranged an excellent clerk-ship with a barrister, I've no doubt before long I shall be one myself, and able to offer Isobel the most secure future and so, sir, I'm asking, sir, if I may have the honor and privilege of your consent to allow me to speak to Isobel of my intention that if she is willing, if she'll have me, she and I shall become engaged to be married not of course right away but as soon as it may be practicable for both of us, meaning, naturally, when I've achieved a certain status in my clerking and she has finished with her schooling which I understand would mean a wait of some time but I don't mind waiting for *her* since she's so, quite so, special and I am absolutely certain, sir, that I shall be, I mean we shall be exemplary in our behaviour, so if you will only agree I'll approach her will you, sir. Please?

The Evening's Ours

Sandra Anne Reinaud

> Freestanding monologue
> Male
> 30s
> Comic

Carl and Polly have thought through every last detail of the surprise party they're throwing for their friend, Sam. But Polly is worried that Sam is on to them. Just in case she's right, Carl coaches her on the fine art of diversionary lying.

CARL:

Okay, let's say he out-and-out asks you: "Polly, you're not planning a surprise party for me, are you?" No sweat. You just need to be prepared.

So, you have three options:

Admit it, replace it with another lie…then make him feel *terrible* about asking: Like: "Yeah, I am, Sam. It's next Tuesday, at 6:00. When you go to pick up your drycleaning, a whole bunch of your friends and loved ones—including grade school friends you haven't seen in years—will jump out from behind the counter. There. Happy? God… you are such a pain."

Flatter him. Like: "Ri-i-i-ght, Sam. Like I could ever surprise *you*! You are too, too sharp for that…I mean, you don't miss a thing! Seriously, I did consider it, for about two seconds…but *when* would I be able to plan a surprise party? We see each other every day, we do *everything* together… Sorry, hon. You're too clever to be the surprise-party type. But that's why we love you."

Or…just make it all about you. A classic diversion. Like: "Of course I'm not planning a party! Oh, wait….Oh, shit… did you *want* one? Oh my god, I'm sorry! I am such a dope. You are so good to me and this is how I repay you. I suck."

See, relax, Polly. You just need to be prepared. And girl, we ARE prepared. Right?

Exit, Pursued by a Bear (#1)

Lauren Gunderson

> Play
> Male
> 27
> Comic

Simon, a North Georgian, is "pretty and strong and bitchy, like a slim cat." His best bud, Nan, duck-taped her abusive husband to a chair and intends to leave him there until he is eaten by a bear. Simon approves. He poses in a red cheerleaders' outfit. Shakes the pom-pom. This is sarcastic, judge-y, mocking, whatevah. Note: "Pregnant pause" is spoken aloud, one of the many delightful quirks of this play-not-pretending-to-be-other-than-a-play.

SIMON:

Yaaaay, he's innocent. He doesn't know what in the world he did wrong. Bless his heart! Pregnant pause.

Now that shit bird has f-ed with my girl. And that does not abide in the house of Simon. Because Nan and I have been righteous friends since we met at the Drama Club Interest Meeting on the first day of middle school. She is my soulmate, y'all. For God sake's, we went to prom together (in a slightly ironic way but we had fun)—*And* she was the first person I came out to and, y'all, she said Jesus loved me even more because I had the courage to be true to the way God made me and God made me pretty fabulous—*And* junior year she played Juliet to my – well I played Balthazar so we didn't really—whatever, it was miscast—the point is we defy category and crap ass husbands.

Now. Let's take a journey into the mind of one Kyle Carter.

Systematic abuse slash desperate need for women that his father and modern buddy comedies taught him ever since his very first beer at age 12, which was quickly followed by a joke about a woman with two black eyes that's supposed to be funny because the punchline is something like "you've already told her twice"—which solidified the neural pathway from whiskey, to funny, to girls-being-hit, to do-what-it-takes-to-feel-like-a-man, to being king, two realizing your kingdom is a cracked driveway in the woods and you're a dream-withered mammal dying of Cheeto-induced heart disease, to hurting my friend, to shame that would be the color of eggplants if things like that we're color-coded, to drinking more, to losing his step, to losing it all, to this very moment right goddamn now.

(Silence. Pompom.)

Exit, Pursued by a Bear (#2)

Lauren Gunderson

> Play
> Male
> 28
> Comic

Kyle, from Georgia, is "a big messy boy, like a dumb dirty dog." He has been duct-taped to a chair by his wife (assisted by a stripper), who has finally had enough of his redneck ways. He addresses the audience directly.

KYLE:

I think we got off on the wrong foot here. I'm not an asshole. For real. Listen to me, I don't know why she's pitching this fit in front of everybody. And I know it's not technically legal but those deer are in my backyard dammit so it's more like a lawn mowing and people don't need permission for that. And people—like—do stuff other people don't like. Like couples. That's how relationships work, goddamnit, and you don't have to duct tape 'em to a damn chair! And I swear I don't know who that other one is who is that?!

You don't believe me. I can tell you're sitting there thinking she might be right about me. That I just might deserve…

Shit. Shitshitshit –

I'll be straight with y'all—I don't know how this is going to and I really don't. She doesn't ever get mad, and she sure don't "act it all out" (which I'm not sure I get what that's about). The point is I don't know what the hell is going on and what the hell I did to make whatever is going on, going on.

I'm trying to say that she's lost it—and we are not safe—and I don't deserve this! Who deserves this!? THERE ARE BEARS OUT THERE—Please Lord Jesus help me—she might actually kill me and I'm really hungry and my head hurts like a bitch and—JESUSLORD come on help me—y'all *know* this is crazy-pleasegod*pleasegodPLEASE.*

Family Meeting Announcing My Recently Published Submission

Tim Cushing

Online magazine post
Male
20s-40s
Comic

Some people just don't understand the awesome accomplishment of an online publication.

MAN:

I'd like to thank you all for coming here on such short notice. I'm aware that many of you had unfinished business elsewhere, especially those of you whose supervisors were left in the lurch by your sudden disappearance.

First of all, I'd like to clear the air: Uncle Chet has not passed away, as many of you might have expected due to his recent health problems or the subject line of my email. (...)

No, this meeting is to draw your attention to my recent publication in a Major Online Publication.

I'm sorry. This hand gesture indicates "air capitalization." I'm trying to emphasize the importance of this journal, which is much harder to do verbally without excessive facial expressions and/or inadvertent spitting. (...)

This major online humor journal has selected my piece to run today, and I'd like for all of you to read it. Yes, I'm sure many of you have never heard of it, but let me assure you, it is a Major Online Publication.

That's right. That means "air caps." (...)

Chet, I specifically requested your presence as you've dodged all other invitations to read my published work. The assertion that you "don't get the internet where you live" won't fly this time. I've got plenty of internet here and I'd like you to go first.

And Carmen, I know you've said repeatedly in the past that you just don't "get" my humor. (...) I'm telling you, Carmen, if you don't "get" this one then I sincerely doubt you know Art Buchwald's body of work quite as well as you think you do.

Now, I've got it open on the computer in the den. I'd like for each of you to take a turn reading it. When you're done, please fill out one of the comment cards I've printed up. Be sure to indicate which line(s) was your favorite. This will be completely anonymous so be candid. I'm especially curious to hear which line(s) you thought were the best.

No, those were "air parentheses." The "air caps" look like this. Go ahead and use that whenever. But not the "air caps." I'm patenting that in case this whole writing thing doesn't pan out.

Fancy Jeans Are the Future of this Company

Pete Reynolds

> Online magazine post
> Male
> 30s-50s
> Comic

The company president addresses his stakeholders with his cutting-edge plan for the future.

PRESIDENT:

Welcome, shareholders, employees, and members of the board. As you know, it has always been the goal of this company not only to turn a profit, but to meet the needs of a changing America. My grandfather built this company on nothing but a dream, elbow grease, seed capital from numerous wealthy investor friends, a $500,000 revolving line of credit from the bank, a second dream telling him to give it all up and become a jazz musician which he wisely ignored, and an extremely lucrative contract with the U.S. Army to make its uniforms for our boys fighting overseas during World War II. He then passed this company along to my father, who hated jazz, so that was never an issue, and who took this company to the skies, making the space-age garments that kept our astronaut heroes safe on their way to the moon and back. (…)

As the needs of our country evolve, so too must we. And if it's not clear to you already, then it will be soon: the future of this company is in fancy jeans. (…)

Now, I'll admit that I am not an expert in elaborately stitched denimwear. I haven't spent years studying the intricacies of back pocket embroidery. I'm no Mr. Fancy Pants walking around the mall … being fancy in his new fancy jeans. I didn't graduate from Fancy University with a major in Pants Studies. It's not like I then went on to get a master's in Advanced Pants Studies at some graduate program, because, like, what else was I going to do with a degree in Pants Studies except keep studying pants because, surprise, surprise, Pants Studies isn't exactly engineering when it comes to learning anything that has real-world applications.

But I do know sales. And I know this great country, and I know that while America's appetite for defense spending and space exploration may wax and wane, its desire for ever fancier jeans never will.

Frank Amends

Halley Feiffer

> Play
> Male
> 20s-30s
> Comic

Frankenstein's monster ("Frank") visits the doctor who created him to confess that he is a newly sober member of Alcoholics Anonymous who would like to make amends for his past harms. Frank wears skinny jeans, bright neon oversized high-tops, and a bright red American Apparel hoodie. The doctor wears a lab coat.

FRANK:

Okay. Well, I guess I'll just...cut to the...I mean, I came here tonight, to, uh—to— *(He mops his brow.)* God, I'm nervous all of a sudden...*(He unfolds a piece of paper.)* "Doctor Frankenstein: Thank you for meeting me here today. I was looking back on past behavior and wanted to set right some wrongs...(*Pushing through; this is very hard for him.*) I was: hard, abrupt, inconsiderate, selfish, unkind, and a murderer. I may have caused you harm while we were cohabitating because I was self-involved and reckless. And a murderer. I regret this behavior.

I appreciate how dedicated you are to your work, and what a good creator you were to me...

I love – I love how you always remembered to change the bolts in my neck when they got rusty...

How you would always try to trim my unibrow—(...) and I wouldn't let you—(...) and you'd be like— "Frank—Frank! you have to prune that thing! You look like the—" (*Cracking up*) —"You look like the walking *dead*, Frank!" Oh em GEE you said that *so* many times!

(*Returning to his letter.*) "Is there anything you would like to say to me? (...) Is there any way I can right these wrongs? The End." (...)

Okay, thanks! I guess I should go call my sponsor. (...) You might know him—his name is Dracula?(...)

No, just kidding, he's this dude from Bay Ridge named Vince.

God Only Knows
Michael Bailey

> Freestanding monologue
> Male
> 30s-50s
> Comic

Mike has ideas on religion and is willing to share them with you. You're welcome.

MIKE:

So I'm sitting in this coffee shop and a guy comes in with his son who looks about three years old, and they sit at the table next to mine, because I'm like a magnet for people hauling small children into coffee shops where virtually EVERYTHING hints that they are not welcome. They were playing Lou Reed, for Christ sake. Apparently, they came from Sunday school because the kid has his Bible study comic in which Jesus looks like a bearded Ralph from *Happy Days*, and Dad asks him what he learned, and the kids says, "We learned about Abraham." Then Dad says, "Tell me what was special about him." And *that* got my attention because even I know that Abraham's major claim to fame was being perfectly willing to slaughter his own son because he thought that's what God wanted, which wouldn't be *my* choice for best Bible starter-story for my preschool boy. Hopefully, the voice in that dad's head skewed a bit more Mr. Rogers, and a bit less Yahweh.

The only religious person who ever made any sense to me was my Grandma, who was a devout Catholic, walked to mass every morning rain or shine, but she didn't feel like she needed to be jerked around by any deities. Once she lost something in her apartment, so she prayed a novena to St. Anthony, the patron saint of lost stuff, and she gave him about a week to find it, and he didn't come through. So she left his statue out on the porch all winter.

Goodbye Charles (#2)

Gabriel Davis

> Play
> Male
> 26
> Comic

A young man has decided to throw himself another bar-mitzvah, and hopes to get it right this time.

DAVID:

No, I'm not here to propose marriage again. You said no and I respect that decision. But I've been thinking a lot about what you said. That I'm not ready, that I need to grow up. I've been thinking about it and I wanted you to know, I think I figured it out.

My bar-mitzvah—my transformation from boy to man at the age of 13. I don't think I got it right. I remember stuttering when I read the Shema. And my chanting, especially during the Haftorah was a little off-key. So I'm thinking, maybe, I didn't enter manhood properly.

But what if I got bar-mitzvahed again? What if I got re-bar-mitzvahed? I could knock my bar-mitzvah out of the synagogue this time.

So I've been studying Hebrew, going to Saturday services, making Gefilte fish from scratch! I can feel it, I'm ready. Ready to pay a mortgage and take out a 401k and father some kids. Tomorrow is my big day. Tomorrow, thirteen years after my first bar-mitzvah I am going to do it again. Tomorrow I will step up on that bema and you will WITNESS my TRANSFORMATION!

So, anyhoo...that's why I'm here. Just wanted to hand deliver this invitation to my bar-mitzvah. And, um...if you could just fill out this little card—chicken or fish. Thanks!

Goodbye Charles (#3)
Gabriel Davis

> Play
> Male
> 20s
> Comic

A fact-checker, against his nature, falls in love.

KENNEDY:

I'm not the kind of guy who spends hundreds on a last-minute flight back to New York, tears across town, then runs up six flights of stairs and knocks on my best friend's girlfriend's door in order to run off and elope with her based on one crazy, thoughtless, inexplicably romantic night.

So what am I doing here, Audrey? I'm not passionate. I'm a fact checker for Christ's sake. And the fact of me—being here—doesn't check out.

I mean, this is the kind of thing that only happens in the movies—and we're not in the movies. We're on McDougal Street, two blocks south of Bleecker—that's where we are. That is an indisputable geographical fact.

We can't do this. Because the fact is you are in a relationship. Because the fact is we just met yesterday. Because the fact is I'm not the kind of guy who falls in love.

But the problem is....see...the problem is...despite every fact I can muster, there's something that still doesn't check out. Because the truth is despite all facts to the contrary...I still love you madly. And it just defies all reason. But I do. And it's not like me. And I don't want to. But I can't help it.

I'm yours, Audrey. Completely, totally, hopelessly, and utterly...yours..

Here's How My Humor Works
Patrick McKay

Online magazine post
Male
20s-30s
Comic

A "comedian" invites his friends to Sidelines Bar & Grill to over-explain his hilarity.

COMEDIAN:

Yo, guys. How's it going? (…) Glad you made it.

Well, I guess I should get started telling you guys how funny I am.

(…) The way my humor works is, someone always comes in and runs through my material ahead of time, just so you know that I'm funny. Otherwise, you won't know. You won't understand my jokes, or when to laugh—(…) and you might end up thinking I'm NOT funny.(…)

Let me give you a quick example. I have this bit on urethral inscriptions. It's hysterical. But you would have no idea that it was hysterical unless my Social Amusement Advance Director did their job first. (…)

It's my SAAD's job to explain the amusement. In this case, that every dude has a urethral inscription, or writing inside the tube that runs up the center of his penis. My SAAD would also explain (…) that urethral inscriptions in gay men run in spirals and are usually Barbra Streisand lyrics. See how that works?

It's hilarious because no one has a urethral inscription, gay or otherwise. They're impossible to acquire.

It's not racist. Gay isn't a race. My SAAD would cover that up front. (…)

Where are you going, Isaac? I just prefer we wait for table service.

Hamish? Headin' out?

You're going up, Isaac? But the waitress…(…)

Look, the only way you're going to know I'm funny when I tell you this stuff is if you're around to hear me tell you I'm funny when I tell you this stuff.

That's just how it works, my humor.

Housekeeping
G. William Zorn

> Play
> Male
> 30s-40s
> Comic

The Hustler teaches his young protégé how to seduce the married man next-door.

HUSTLER:

Next time you catch him lookin', don't let him see that you see him. Shirt off, hot and sweaty, maybe scratch yer balls a couple times. The vibration of the mower gettin' to ya. But, aw, yer done. Grass is cut. What now, you say? *Gosh, it's hot. Maybe I should try to cool down a bit. Oh, look. The hose. That'll do the trick.* After a month o' that, if he ain't full-on jerkin' off in that window, I'll eat my hat. Now, this next part's where ya bring the party to where he lives. On the fourth Saturday, after you got him all worked up, put the mower away, but instead of goin' inside, wander on over to his house. You knock on the door and when he eyes your sixteen-year old, wet, half-naked bod in front of him, tell him you're trying to make some extra cash and is there anything he might *need done* around the house. Talk about your porn movie.

Some people are good at math, I do this. *I* should write a book.

I and You

Lauren Gunderson

Play
Male
17
Comic

Anthony, African-American, shows up in Caroline's bedroom with homework, poster board, and a snack. Caroline, white, ("small but mighty. Like a dachshund.") has liver disease and is confined to her bedroom. She was not expecting this stranger, a student from school, to enter her sanctuary. And if you have not read this play, go read it RIGHT NOW because it is THAT good. Best surprise ending EVAH! We'll wait. Off you go.

ANTHONY:

Your mom just gave me cookies (…) and she said you were in your room, and she said I should just come up.

(…) OK. I'm Anthony. Which I might have mentioned. And I have our assignment for American lit, which she was supposed to email you about. And I didn't hear back from her or from you, so finally, like an idiot, I just came over, *in person*, which people still do. So please, *please*, can you calm down, pitch in, or at least sign the poster so it *looks* like we worked together.

(…) WhoaWhoaWhoa, dachshund. There is no scheme. There is a guy with a snack. I am that guy and this is that snack and there is an email and you should check it and maybe find some super clear information and maybe—just maybe—though it seems you really like the high-stakes perspective—try to de-freak yourself out.

(…) I have school in the morning, and I'm sorry you're sick, and I'm sorry you're impossible, but you can take your *small-dog rage* and put it on YouTube because I don't actually have time for this—*OhMyGodGirlsAreAwful.*

I Feel Like NPR Doesn't Like My New Radio Show Idea

Dan Kennedy

> Online magazine post
> Male
> 40s-50s
> Comic

A guy pitches a new radio show idea to public radio executives. Hey, Ira Glass had to start somewhere, right?

MAN:

Hi, hi there. Little nervous. I love your offices here. Okay, so…

It seems these days everyone has a podcast or public radio show. But nobody's doing a public radio show where the host sits in chain restaurants in the middle of America, listening to Hall and Oates, Kansas, and Blue Oyster Cult, wondering what went wrong. Yet. Can you even point to one example; because I feel like you can't look me in the eye and tell me you've already got a show with a middle-aged man listening to music in a steak house across the parking lot from an Old Navy asking strangers questions like "Can I crash at your place?" and "Where does time go?" If you guys already have a show like that, I'll get up and walk out of your office here, no harm, no foul. Just look me in the eye and say, "Oh, yeah, we got a thing called Man Rambler or whatever, comes on during the weekends, a guy sits in the bar of a Red Lobster listening to Skynrd and asking people rhetorical questions like, "Is it enough to dream and visualize things, or have we been misled by fairytales and self-help books that never mention hard work, dead ends, and years spent struggling?" If you've got that show already, I'll hold my hands up, tell you to have a great day, and that's the end of it. But I'm looking around the room here and I'm not seeing anybody flapping their gums about having anything like this on the air, so I'm gonna keep going. How many people come in here in a month and pitch you shows? Tons, I bet. I can hear them now: "Oh, hi, I'm some Einstein and I was thinking I could host a show where I yammer about super smart things, how's that sound?" And you guys are sitting there thinking, 'Uh, pretty sure we got that covered, Sherlock.' and you feel bad for that person. But I'm looking around the room right now and I'm seeing a lot of jaws hitting the floor, I'm seeing wide-eyed stares, you're all looking at each other then back at me, and I'm guessing that means we're on to something good, so let's keep jamming here.

Jesus Hates Me (#1)

Wayne Lemon

> Play
> Male
> 30s-40s
> Comic

Trane, a Stetson-wearing, African-American lawman in a small Texas town, lies on his stomach in a hospital bed, having shot himself in the rear end.

TRANE:

I better get a motherfucking medal.

Son of a bitch kept doubling back, trying to throw me off. Get lost in traffic. Blend in. Any idea how many Winnebagos on the road this time of year? Bunch a old people from Minnesota, all blue veins and false teeth, talking about how their bones are chilled and they down here to get warm and my ain't the wildflowers pretty? I'm like I ain't got time for this, I got to find me a child molester and have they seen him? They all interested until I describe the little girl, find out she's Vietnamese then it's have another cup a coffee officer and my it must be difficult being the only Negro on the force. Patting my hand and shit as if to make sure it's really black. Finally get a call there's a Winnebago matching the description parked in the middle of that old abandoned drive-in out on the county line. Just sitting there, like they waiting for the movie to start. I roll up silent, identify myself, draw my service revolver, get ready to go in. Strictly by the book. Don't want the son of a bitch to walk 'cause I screwed the bust.

Winnebago wasn't even locked. Walked right in. Motherfucker sitting there watching Full House on the TV. Little girl in his lap, eating a corn dog, laughing. He sees me, starts bawling 'bout how he hadn't touched her, just gave her a bubble bath, painted her toenails. Gets all hysterical, begging me not to arrest him. Scaring the shit out of the little girl. Finally hit him just to shut him up. Holstering my weapon when it went off.

Listen to me, man. I like being a cop. I intend to stay a cop. I actually do some good for people, people white folks don't give a damn about. People like that little girl. But if the truth comes out,

I'm through. No way they let me do the one thing I can do. And I know you know how that feels.

Be amazed what you can live with once you shot yourself in the ass. You sure that looks like I got hit with a tire iron? Better hit me again, just to make sure.

Jesus Hates Me (#2)
Wayne Lemon

> Play
> Male
> 27
> Comic

> *Boone, 27, a Texan womanizer and loose cannon, gets religion.*
> *For a little while, anyway.*

BOONE:

Listen bro, we've been friends a long time — No?

Oh, I get it. Reject me before I reject you. It's cool. I can take it. But I want you to know something. I've always believed a man needs just three things in life—pussy, beer...and pussy. But last night, after you showed up and tried to pull my arms and legs off then passed out, your mama and me sat out here talking. First it was about all the bitterness you carry around inside, then about miniature golf and its purpose in the grand scheme of creation...

And I don't know, maybe it was the moonlight, maybe it was the warm sense of assurance in her voice or the fact that I was drunk off my ass, but for the first time in my life it started to make sense. What it's all about. Why we're here.

To love one other. So let me just say...I love you, man...in a strictly heterosexual way...even though we're both standing here in your underwear...semierect. And she loves you, too. Don't ever doubt that. Doesn't mean to be the way she is.

I'm not scared, not anymore. Not since last night. All my fears, my doubts, I laid them down right there, at the foot of that cross. Or maybe it was there. Or over there. Somewhere in the general vicinity—like I said, I was beat up from the feet up. The only thing I'm sure of is I'm no longer frozen in those headlights of yours. I have found the truth, man, and now I *am free.*

[ETHAN: So you'll be going home?]

Fuck no, I'm not going home. Just 'cause I'm free don't mean I wanna die. I mean, let's be practical. He ain't gonna hop down off [the cross] and stop a bullet, dude.

Jesus Hates Me (#4)

Wayne Lemon

Play
Male
27
Comic

Boone, 27, is an affable loser in a small town in Texas. He talks to Lizzy, part-owner of a bar. He's been drinking. Duh.

BOONE:

Northern bands are pussy, southern bands are killer, the South deserved to win the Civil War. Now I know you're wondering where the British stand in all this. Gonna side with the North and you know why? They're ass jockeys, every one of 'em! Reason they refuse to free Ireland—need the Irish to impregnate their women otherwise they'd never reproduce as a race.

God, I hope *[I'm drunk.]*

Got fired today. Everything I've worked so hard for, struggled to build for so long. A little piece of something to call my own... gone, over, just like that.

[Yeah, it was my first day, but] It was more than a job. I was finally able to satisfy my inner yearning to create. [Blowing holes in the ground to put in swimming pools.] Holy Christ I loved it. The feeling was indescribable. Like coming only with dynamite and big chunks of dirt.

Technically I might've blown up a dog. Old Man Jennings'. Tossed a stick of dynamite into the pit. Golden retriever tore past me like it was after a rabbit or something. Managed to find most of him, shoveled him under a tarp in the back of my truck, planned to bury him after dark, only Jennings shows up, goes to take a leak unaware Queenie's head blew a hole in the Porta-John and is sitting there in the urinal. Son of a bitch sees it, strokes out, now everyone's acting like it's my fault. Talking about bringing charges. Animal cruelty. Like I'd purposefully train a dog to fetch dynamite. Never woulda happened if his tennis ball hadn't gone up on the roof.

The Knave of Hearts
Louise Saunders

> Play
> Male
> 30s-40s
> Comic

The knave has been caught. This is his reply when asked why he stole Violetta's tarts. Seriously, who can blame him?

KNAVE:

All my life I have had a craving for tarts of any kind. There is something in my nature that demands tarts—something in my constitution that cries out for them—and I obey my constitution as rigidly as does the Chancellor seek to obey his. I was in the garden reading, as is my habit, when a delicate odor floated to my nostrils, a persuasive odor, a seductive, light brown, flaky odor, an odor so enticing, so suggestive of tarts fit for the gods—- that I could stand it no longer. It was stronger than I. With one gesture I threw reputation, my chances for future happiness, to the winds, and leaped through the window. The odor led me to the oven; I seized a tart, and, eating it, experienced the one perfect moment of my existence. After having eaten that one tart, my craving for other tarts has disappeared. I shall live with the memory of that first tart before me forever, or die content, having tasted true perfection.

Ladies and Gentlemen, the Rain
Will Eno

> Play
> Male
> 30s-40s
> Comic

The Gentleman is making a video for the purpose of employing a dating service.

GENTLEMAN:

I have different interests. I enjoy not traveling. I don't speak any second language. Fine dining, live music, and cinema can come and go. I stay out of museums. I stay away from home. I don't have a favorite food, but I guess I like cholesterol...In the summer, I like not having the heat on. In the winter, I like to not sit in front of a fan. I try to look on the bright side. I am not, as I look around myself, currently bleeding.

(...) I have faults, obviously. Some weak points are my knees and back. And I don't have any patience for things that take a long time. Although, it should be said, I'm usually very deeply just waiting. Bugs fly in my mouth sometimes, because I'm just standing there, full of want, full of open-mouthed wonder. I stay like that long enough to give them time to fly out, because although unknowing, I am not unkind.

(Brief pause.)

I like walking. I'll run, if I have to. Or stay still. But you're never going to find me shaking on the floor, biting into my own hand, and crying out into the daylight. Except, sometimes. But really only rarely, on those occasions.

Love, Honor and Obey
Scott Hermes

> Play
> Male
> 25-50
> Comic

If you deliver this as if a fervent preacher, you'll rule the room.

HUSBAND:

Goddamn, my wife makes me feel sexy.

Now, I don't know how I look to you, you may not even be attracted to men. And you may think I look like some kind of freak, thing that crawled out from under a rock, well maybe if you were the last man on earth, but goddamn, my wife makes me feel sexy.

Look, I don't know what's wrong with her. Why when she looks at me, she gets that look, yes, that look, "you've got the look, you've got the look of love"—sexy, dammit. I don't know why this particular combination of eyes ears nose lips teeth smile chicken legs butt dick back chest and arms tongue gut neck make her loop the loop, but it does. And when she says c'mere, you bet your ass, your bottom dollar, your goddamn farm, and the mother-fucking moon, that I drop what I am doing and run, jump, skip to my Lou, my darling, my Clementine, my baby, baby, baby, baby, baby, baby please.

Goddamn, my wife makes me feel sexy.

Mazel Tov Boys
Ty Samuels

Freestanding monologue
Male
40s-50s
Comic

Fighting for the right to legally marry his partner of 22 years was the easy part for Stephen. Now he must convince his dear friend Beth to let him and Jason make the wedding a quiet affair.

STEPHEN:

We are *not* releasing doves.

We are not planting a tree, we're not stomping on a glass, and please—at our ages—no hora. We're not registering at Bloomingdale's or anywhere, for that matter. Come on, Beth: Jason and I set up house together more than twenty years ago. We don't need a blender; we're downsizing.

I understand that you'd like to dance at our wedding, and that's very sweet, but that's just not us. You know that we've both been highly critical—or at least suspect—of the whole institution anyway. Since college; before even. We grew up good little feminists. This is just about leveling the playing field. And saving money on our taxes.

So we're going to the courthouse, signing the paper, going out afterwards, that's it. Just join us for dinner, OK? Believe me, people will be relieved we're not doing a big wedding. Especially in New York, folks are just happy knowing they don't need to show up.

But if you're absolutely compelled—well, pick up dinner. There, happy?

A Meteorologist Works Out Some Personal Issues During His Forecast

Pete Reynolds

> Online magazine post
> Male
> 30s
> Comic

You've heard of bringing your work home? This guy brings home to work.

METEOROLOGIST:

A quick glance at the Channel 3 Weather Map shows widespread temperatures well into the mid-90s, with the heat index likely to tip over into triple digits (...) It's going to be terrible, folks. (...) Enough to make you hate yourself for all the things you were too afraid to say to Karen.

The current mark is a toasty 98 degrees, set on this date back in 2005, which also happens to be the last time Karen said that she loved me.

Look, if you want me to tell you that there will be a pleasant breeze, or that last night's showers cleared out some of the mugginess, well, I'm not going to say those things, because those things are lies. Unlike Kevin O'Dell and the Channel 6 Weather Squad, and Karen when she says the word "forever," I'm not in the business of lying, or of telling you that it's not going to be very, very uncomfortable to be outside. It is. It's going to feel like you're wearing a sweatshirt made out of Alfredo sauce. You're going to hate it.

Probably there will be mosquitoes, too.

"Some relief from the heat and humidity is on the way, though," is something I'd love to be able to say to you now. But I can't. This heat isn't going away, and neither is the pain of hearing your daughter call another man "Dad," especially when that man is Kevin O'Dell from the Channel 6 Weather Squad.

Be sure to check back with us for more updates on this dreary hellscape of a day, during which you will consider ripping the very flesh from your bones just for the ventilation it brings.

Back to you, Karen.

A Midsummer Night's Dream (#2)

William Shakespeare

> Play
> Male
> 35-45
> Comic

Duke Theseus makes the comparison between those in love and the mentally disturbed.

THESEUS:

Lovers and madmen have such seething brains,
Such shaping fantasies, that apprehend
More than cool reason ever comprehends.
The lunatic, the lover and the poet
Are of imagination all compact:
One sees more devils than vast hell can hold,
That is, the madman: the lover, all as frantic,
Sees Helen's beauty in a brow of Egypt:
The poet's eye, in fine frenzy rolling,
Doth glance from heaven to earth, from earth to heaven;
And as imagination bodies forth
The forms of things unknown, the poet's pen
Turns them to shapes and gives to airy nothing
A local habitation and a name.
Such tricks hath strong imagination,
That if it would but apprehend some joy,
It comprehends some bringer of that joy;
Or in the night, imagining some fear,
How easy is a bush supposed a bear!

The Monologue Show (From Hell) (#1)
Don Zolidis

> Play
> Male
> Teen
> Comic

Bradley took a high school theatre class because it was supposed to be fun. Nobody told him he had to actually do stuff, for like, a grade.

BRADLEY:

Anyway, ANYWAY, my monologue is about lawn gnomes. Anybody gonna laugh about that? This is a very serious monologue. People will be crying at the end of it. All right? It's beautiful.

So this one time me and my friends were gonna steal garden gnomes. I got this friend named Jamison, anyone know him? He's insane. He's a deviant, right? But he's got this truck and he's like, "Dude, yes!" He doesn't like to use a lot of words, you know? 'Cause he's like poetic and stuff? So I'm like, "What?" And he's like, "Gnomes."

And I'm just like, "Let's do it!" (…) So we go out in Jamison's truck. (…) This time I see the gnome. Just one. Jamison is like, "You've got to steal it 'cause I'm on probation for stealing garden gnomes." And I'm like on probation too, for something totally unrelated—so glad my probation officer isn't here today. Not here, right? Officer Dooley are you here? Not here? Okay cool. So I sprint to the gnome. And I'm like, "YOLO"—I say that a lot—and I grab the gnome, and I fall right over. The gnome is chained to the ground. I'm serious. There's like a leg manacle thing, and the gnome is chained down.

These people have no trust. That's a shame, right? Like, this is our society. People are chaining their garden gnomes down 'cause they're paranoid. It's sad. So I'm like, "Abort! Abort!" Lights come on. Motion lights. There's like a hundred cops waiting for us. Alright maybe not a hundred. Maybe like one, whatever. (…) So then I'm like, "Drive! Drive!" I jump in the truck like I'm in an action movie. (…) Boom. Over the curb. Over like thirty hedges or whatever—people got hedges everywhere, like are these supposed to stop trucks com running over their lawns—they don't work—

we're like, bam over the curb, bam over another curb, tires are like on fire and smoking, women are throwing babies out of our way.

We look back. The cop didn't even chase us. High five.

It was awesome. Thank you.

My Carpet Liquidation Center Really is Going Out of Business This Time

Patrick McKay

Online magazine post
Male
50s
Comic

You've heard the ads, you've seen the stores. Meet the guy.

LIQUIDATOR:

I'd always wanted to be a carpet liquidator. Way back when I first opened this place, I said, "Man, this is it. I've joined a community. I'm staying here forever." Then, it happened. Completely out of the blue, my carpet liquidation center that'd been going out of business for 11 straight years, was suddenly going out of business! And I never saw it coming! (…)

Sure, I feel like I let the neighborhood down. That's only natural. When a carpet liquidation center enters the community, people expect it to be around for a long, long time. Carpet liquidators that are going out of business aren't supposed to just leave. It's bad form. And can really screw with a liquidator's reputation.

But while closing the doors where my kids grew up, where my best memories were forged, where my carbon footprint was ostentatiously stamped, is devastating to my psyche, my family, and my assortment of miniature forklifts, something good can still come of it.

Namely, huge savings! Because this isn't your everyday liquidation sale! This carpet liquidation center actually is going out of business! 99% off everything, motherfuckers! Free installation until I skip zip codes! If you don't buy it, I'll goddamn burn it!!!!!!

Make sure you come see me at my new location just off North Fairfax and Selma Avenue.

The Norwegians (#3)

C. Denby Swanson

Play
Male
30s-40s
Comic

Tor, a Norwegian hitman living in Minnesota, commingles his love of baseball with his chosen profession.

TOR:

Here's what I'm thinking in that moment. The moment of ending a life. It is the single most important moment they will ever have. The end. It's an event they will get to experience only once. Only once. They don't expect it to be happening now. But it is. It is. It is happening now. I want it to go well. Is it possible that a baseball bat isn't the best choice? Might seem that way. Sure. To an outsider. In 1991, the Minnesota Twins won the World Series. It was a magical season. Just magical. We haven't had one like it since. And I was there for the whole thing. The Twins and the Braves were the first two teams in Major League history to start out last and end up first. It's so biblical. Almost prophetic. So restrained. And so—so—so Norwegian. And the last shall be first. So deeply Norwegian. It took the whole seven games. Four at home. We could have been nice and come in second. We could have been true to our nature. But we got up our nerve and we actually won. That's the way that I think about growing the business as well. The Norwegians could be second in market share. Second in revenues. Third, even. And that would be fine. Because inside, we would know ourselves champions, gracious to the competition, we would know it in our hearts. We would even be nice about it. Or we could beat the living crap out of the other team, and win. I love the Minnesota Twins. I love them with all my heart. And this is their winning bat.

The Offer
Rand Higbee

Freestanding monologue
Male
20s-30s
Comic

Mark needs to work on his proposing skills.

MARK:

Let's face it, Sally. I'm a loser. I can't hold onto a job much less find one in the first place. And if I did have a job, well, I probably wouldn't work very hard at it. And no, I'm no stranger to the bottle or to the inside of a jail cell. And yes, there are a few more warrants out there to take care of. But don't you see, Sally? With you by my side I'd be a new man! There's no telling how high I could fly!

And yes, I confess, I did sleep with your sister. A few times. But it was just Becky! I never touched Gina at all! And that's the truth! But Becky, why, she just looks so much like you! And you know how much I love you! So what was I supposed to do?

(Gets down on one knee and takes out a ring box.)

And no, there's no ring in here right now. Who am I fooling? I couldn't afford to buy a ring. But if you would borrow me the money, Sally, I would buy such a ring as to make all your friends green with envy. I would get you the best engagement ring your money could buy. Come on. What do you say, Sally?

Overruled (#2)
George Bernard Shaw

> Play
> Male
> 30s-40s
> Comic

Gregory and Mrs. Juno are at the beginning of their affair. He is quite content, thank you very much, but may be about to get an earful.

GREGORY:

Do you know why half the couples who find themselves situated as we are now behave horridly? It's because they have nothing else to do, and no other way of entertaining each other. They don't know what it is to be alone with a woman who has little beauty and less conversation. What is a man to do? She can't talk interestingly; and if he talks that way himself she doesn't understand him. He can't look at her: if he does, he only finds out that she isn't beautiful. Before the end of five minutes they are both hideously bored. There's only one thing that can save the situation; and that's what you call being horrid. With a beautiful, witty, kind woman, there's no time for such follies. It's so delightful to look at her, to listen to her voice, to hear all she has to say, that nothing else happens. That is why the woman who is supposed to have a thousand lovers seldom has one; whilst the stupid, graceless animals of women have dozens.

Paper Towels
Daniel Guyton

> Freestanding monologue
> Male
> 26-40
> Comic

Frankie confesses to a friend about an embarrassing crime he committed.

FRANKIE:

I'm a...I clean pools. I used to be a kindergarten teacher. But now I'm...I clean pools. *(Beat.)* And fountains too. I was a good teacher, but...they caught me stealing towels from the children's washroom, and...*(Beat.)* Paper. Paper towels. I used to drink a lot of coffee in my office. And...I would spill a lot, you know? In-inevitably. So I would steal the towels from the children's washroom. And...and I would come out with these giant wads of paper products, just...stacks and stacks of them. You know, in...in case something spilled, or whatever. And I...and for the longest time, they blamed this kid named Michael who was five years old. And I don't know why they blamed him 'cause he was always dirty, so it's not like he was using them. But...I didn't want to say anything. In case...you know. I mean...he's just a kid. If he goes down, who cares? But I got my whole career ahead of me, so I can't go down just for stealing paper towels. But then one day there was a flood. The entire school was flooded. Some water pipe exploded. Or... the sewage line or something. And the principal came in to assess the damage. And then he saw my office. With all the paper towels on the shelves, and...boxes on the floor. They said I had stolen over 2,000 dollars' worth of paper products. *(Beat.)* Of course, my office was the driest in the building, but...that didn't matter to them. They had to let me go.

Phone Conference
Michael Bailey

> Freestanding monologue
> Male
> 35+
> Comic

A teacher discusses a student's behavior with a clueless parent.

TEACHER:

I'm sorry to hear that Jeffery is upset about English class today. I think we're all a bit dismayed.

Yes, I did hear Jeffery's version of the events as he related them to our principal.

Well, to be fair, he did leave out some key details. Primarily, the parts about overturning his desk, throwing his crumpled test paper in my face, and calling me an asshole.

Yes Ma'am, I actually *do* think those are relevant details. I'm sorry to hear that Jeffery feels that he's being singled out for discipline.

Yes, we do seem to be frequently in conflict.

Well…that's a bit like asking a fireman why he only charges into the *burning* houses.

No, Ma'am I'm not trying to be funny.

Yes, Jeffery is currently failing English.

Well, it's rather challenging to diagnose Jeffery's particular writing issues, because as we near the end of the term, I have yet to receive any samples to examine. After school tutoring has always been available.

I'm sure he *is very* busy. I'm familiar with the sensation.

No, Ma'am I'm not trying to be funny.

What can he do to pass at this point? I don't typically offer extra credit, but even if I did, at this point Jeffery would have to… publish a novel.

Yes, Ma'am, I *was* trying to be funny that time. How did I do?

The Proposal
Anton Chekhov

Play
Male
30s-40s
Comic

Soon after Lamov proposes to his neighbor's daughter, the two begin to argue, which has ill effects on Lamov's health.

LAMOV:

It's cold...I'm trembling all over, just as if I'd got an examination before me. The great thing is, I must have my mind made up. If I give myself time to think, to hesitate, to talk a lot, to look for an ideal, or for real love, then I'll never get married...Brr!...It's cold! Natalya Stepanovna is an excellent housekeeper, not bad-looking, well-educated...What more do I want? But I'm getting a noise in my ears from excitement. And it's impossible for me not to marry...In the first place, I'm already 35—a critical age, so to speak. In the second place, I ought to lead a quiet and regular life....I suffer from palpitations, I'm excitable and always getting awfully upset...At this very moment my lips are trembling, and there's a twitch in my right eyebrow...But the very worst of all is the way I sleep. I no sooner get into bed and begin to go off when suddenly something in my left side—gives a pull, and I can feel it in my shoulder and head...I jump up like a lunatic, walk about a bit, and lie down again, but as soon as I begin to get off to sleep there's another pull! And this may happen twenty times...

Quake (#1)
Melanie Marnich

> Play
> Male
> 30s
> Comic

> *Over and over, Brian denies evidence of his affair, then confesses in a rush. He hangs up the phone, and...*

BRIAN:

Wrong number.
Really weird.
Um. I dunno.
I dunno.
I dunno.
No.
No.
I think you're really paranoid.
Lucy—
(In one breath, as one word:) It didn't mean anything It was only once No I don't love her It was a mistake I never saw her before I'll never do it again It didn't mean anything It was only once No I don't love her It was a mistake I never saw her before I'll never do it again It didn't mean anything It was only once I'll never do it again.

Give me another chance.
I'll make it up to you. I swear. It didn't mean anything, ever.
I'll never do it again.
It was only once. Lucy?
Lucy?

Quake (#2)
Melanie Marnich

> Play
> Male
> 30s
> Comic

Lucy is in search of the love of her life. She meets Jock.

JOCK:

You're a real sport, Lucy.

I mean, we just met last night. And when you said you wanted to do the whole tour with me, well…

I thought it was just the rum, tequila, ad vermouth talking. But when I saw you in the Frunken Splat Ball Games…

I thought, "This gal can really take a beating!"

Did I meant ion my last girlfriend raced mountain bikes?

Amazing. [She] could pee standing straight up. Which made her great to travel with.

Could ride 80 miles without breaking a sweat.

Hasn't menstruated in seven years. Body like a machine. I think you two would hit it off.

I really like it when sweat gets in my eyes. It burns. You know why it burns? Because there's salt in sweat and salt burns your eyes. Like it burns an open sore. Burning is good. Like it when it burns. Good burn. Good.

Oh yeah. Feel that burn.

Oh yeah.

[Are we there yet?]

Depends where "there" is, Lucy. When you live the life of a jock, "there" is never here. There is always…out there.

If you want to ride with me, Lucy, you'll keep riding. You'll learn to change a tire without slowing down. You'll learn to eat without chewing. you'll learn to sleep without closing your eyes. You'll learn to rest without stopping. It's a great way of life, Lucy.

Keep riding, Lucy. Keep riding. Body is a machine. Oil chain. Shift gears. Burn is good. Good burn, good. You're slowing down, Lucy. Pick it up.

Romeo and Juliet
William Shakespeare

> Play
> Male
> 20+
> Comic

Mercutio is looking for Romeo and, believing his friend is just within earshot, uses jests to get Romeo's attention.

MERCUTIO:

Romeo! Humours! Madman! Passion! Lover!
Appear thou in the likeness of a sigh.
Speak but one rhyme and I am satisfied.
Cry but "Ay me!" Pronounce but "love" and "dove".
Speak to my gossip Venus one fair word,
One nickname for her purblind son and heir,
Young Adam Cupid, he that shot so trim
When King Cophetua loved the beggar maid!
He heareth not, he stirreth not, he moveth not.
The ape is dead, and I must conjure him.
I conjure thee by Rosaline's bright eyes,
By her high forehead and her scarlet lip,
By her fine foot, straight leg, and quivering thigh,
And the demesnes that there adjacent lie,
That in thy likeness thou appear to us!

Seven Stages of an Affair
Lorraine Forrest-Turner

> Play
> Male
> 20s
> Comic

Tony, British, 20s, contemplates that age-old question, "Why do men screw around?"

TONY:

Why do guys screw around? *(Pause.)* Because they can. Oh, come on, no guy lies on his deathbed thinking, "I wish I'd slept with less women." *(Pause.)* Unless of course he's dying of syphilis or something.

OK, maybe that's an oversimplification, but I tell you, I have thought about his long and hard and I still haven't come up with a better answer. I've been through it all. "My wife doesn't understand me." "I was denied the breast as a baby." "I am driven by the biological urge to plant my seeds in as many different wombs a possible."

None of them add up. Linda does understand me. I was suckled until I was fourteen months old. And I always use a condom.

The trouble with me is I *like* women. No honestly, I really like women. I like the way they look, the way they smell, the way they feel. I like the way they talk, the way they get inside your head and make you feel good about yourself. (…) No, the way I look at it, spend two hours with some bloke and you come away knowing why Arsenal lost 2-1 and why your pension is worth half what you thought it was. Spend two hours with a beautiful woman and you don't give a toss either way.

No, the big question for me isn't why do guys screw around, it's why do they stop?

Stark Naked

Georges Feydeau

Translated by Charles Marowitz

> Play
> Male
> 40+
> Comic

Ventroux, an aspiring politician, apologizes for his inappropriate wife.

VENTROUX:

I cannot possibly express how mortified I am, 'sieur Himmelfaahr. *(He makes a point of pronouncing it correctly.)* The fact is my wife is a fanciful creature who suffers from delusions from time to time. It runs in her family, I fear. Her mother was a certified lunatic—or so her father told me—although he himself was under the impression that he was the reincarnation of Napoleon Bonaparte. (…) It is just incredible the things that pop into her head out of her mouth. "Low-brow beady-eyed rodent ..." is really one of her more extraordinary concoctions. At other times, of course, she behaves quite normally. And you must forgive my wife the manner in which she presented herself. I can assure you she's not in the habit of walking around like that. It is, of course, quite warm today which almost—but not quite—excuses her inexcusable behavior. You felt her hands I'm sure. It is very humid today. Here, just feel mine *(Takes one of Himmelfaahr's hands between his own.)* Quite damp as you see. *(Himmelfaahr withdraws his hand and wipes it on his shirt.)* And quite unpleasant.

The Unkempt Yard
Hal Corley

> Play
> Male
> 20s
> Comic

Axton, a Southern lawn boy for a suburban gay couple, explains his unique M.O.

AXTON:

You get an MBA. Go to the Met. Sleep through British plays. Giggle at musicals y'all call "a hoot." Sit on charity boards. Campaign for Liz Warren. But jus' *miss* things. *I'm* a graduate of the worst high school in the south. Study Hall the only honors elective. Got Appalachian roots. Front porch-squattin', rag doll-makin' grannies. Tobaccy-spittin' banjo-strummin' cousins. Toothless uncles who still brew still-swill. My red state DNA produces dull-eyed babies with pitiful IQs. Yet I'm a kinda savant. Possess another kinda wisdom. A cosmic aptitude bestowed only on the dirt-poor assumed to be dumb as bricks: the gift of anthropological second sight. See, for decades now, my people have practiced what I call the Anti-Norma Rae Syndrome. Pointy heads don't come our way to teach us shit. Uh-uh, Honey, *we* infiltrate *y'all*'s backyards. We're there, with our embarrassin' blue-collar ways but inbred savvy to reveal The Truth when y'all got your blinders on. I show up when you need some marginalized nobody to teach you everything you're too messed-up to see for yourselves. So it don't matter if I like to haul branches. I'm here to inspire instead. Is there a bit of the *oracle* about me? Y'all got to wait for that. That's what we deliver, too. Suspense. Into dreary lives that got none. *(He winks knowingly.)*

Urine Trouble Now

Daniel Guyton

> Play
> Male
> 60s
> Comic

Mr. Gibbons is interviewing a new employee for a job. It appears the new employee has substituted his urine sample for that of a Komodo Dragon. This leads Mr. Gibbons to expound upon his own youthful shenanigans.

MR. GIBBONS:

Well… let's just say that I was a bit of a cut-up myself when I was in Harvard. *(He stands and crosses to the window)* Why, I remember one time my classmates and I, we… *(He chuckles fondly)* Well, we engaged in a brown-acid party. Are you familiar with those, Mr. Grayson? *(Beat.)* See, back in the 60's we had this thing called brown acid. There was white acid too, of course, and…blue acid. But the brown acid was very dangerous. My roommate Darren took a trip on brown acid once that he still hasn't recovered from. He thinks he's the president of Paraguay. Anyway, that's neither here nor there. The point is, some of these youthful pastimes can be very dangerous, Mr. Grayson. They may seem fun and intoxicating at the moment. Full of strange adventures. Riding a caterpillar across the east side of Boston for instance. Exposing one's self in the center of Harvard Square to the…President of Paraguay. It's titillating to be sure. But it's certainly not appropriate in a place of business. Eventually, I reached an age where I was forced to put aside my youthful shenanigans. And so should you, Mr. Grayson. See, I became an entrepreneur. The first person in history to sell Sudafed over the telephone. I branched out into diet pills, homeopathic remedies, St. John's Wort, hand creams. You can buy Viagra without a prescription, but only with 1-800-MED-ICIN. "Leave off the last E for Expensive!" *(He chuckles to himself.)* Yes, we generate a quarter of a million dollars a year in sales revenue here in our little operation, and I need someone I can trust! Now, I don't mind you having a little…fun at a bachelor party now and then. Heck, there may be times when I'll need you to…sample some of our merchandise here and there. But to trade in your urine sample for that of a…cold blooded monitor lizard is reprehensible in my opinion. Not to mention they make terrible pets. But look, I personally don't see any point in having my employees take a urine sample any more than you do. What you do on your own time is your own business. As long as you can perform here, that's all that matters to me. However, the FDA has its requirements. And I… do have certain share-holders to answer to. So what do you say I accidentally "lose" these test results here… *(He tears up the sheets of paper and throws them away.)* And have you take another one? *(He hands GRAYSON an empty cup.)* What's the matter? *(He takes the cup back.)* I see. *(Beat.)* Do you have any more lies you wish to tell me, Mr. Grayson? *(Small pause.)* No? Well, that's too bad. Because I can really use someone in my PR department who can lie to the FDA for me. *(He holds out a bag of pills.)* OxyContin? *(He takes one of the pills himself.)* Ah, now that's the good stuff.

Welcome to Caleb's Humane Meats

Dan Kennedy

> Online magazine post
> Male
> 40+
> Comic

If you care about your meat (and really, why wouldn't you?), you'll want to buy from Caleb's Humane Meats.

CALEB:

Let us just come right out and say it: we're not your father's butchers. We're attractive men who can barely have sex without feeling guilty. We're people who have led entire lives not competing for anything because we can feel the pain of anyone who has to lose because of our having needed to win so badly—and we're butchers. (…)

Okay…Let me tell you why you can feel good about eating the cuts you buy from us: All of our meats are raised in the most humane conditions possible. The animals have space to roam, to purchase cars they hate to drive, to compromise, second guess decisions they've made, sit in bars, try to get over feelings with sex and food, hang around the town where they went to high school and try to recapture the spark in their work, watch years fly by, and travel to the same cities over and over again, wondering if they've added up to anything they had hoped to. They're allowed to sleep in, eat candy, get lost in vague fantasies about marrying friends or colleagues, and to basically make mistakes with all their heart. (…) They're well-reviewed writers and artists who have resonated with their audience and fulfilled fans' needs, if not sales projections. They fly first class often enough to make them think it's all leading somewhere. But here's the best part: our animals aren't killed by farmers or butchers. That's right, we let the animals kill themselves…slowly…over years of relatively small, bad decisions. So you can feel good in knowing they are killed the same way you and I are.

Why is No One Downloading My Sex Tape?
Pasha Malla

> Online magazine post
> Male
> 30s-50s
> Comic

Question asked...and answered.

MAN:

Who doesn't love the words "free sex tape"? Seriously, I'm wondering, because it seems to be a lot of people. See, literally no one—not a single human being, living or dead, gay, straight or other—has downloaded my sex tape.

Confusing....

Maybe there's some misunderstanding about the level of hotness of my sex tape. To clarify: it's insanely hot—(...)

So why no downloads—not even one? You'd think that someone—even by accident!—might click the link. It just doesn't make sense.

A lot of people ask, or I imagine they might: "Why would I want to watch a video of a sad, hairy guy masturbating in a canoe?" While I won't stoop so low as to answer this question, I'll answer it with another question: "Shut up, 'doctor'!"

Can I just say something about doctors, quick? Or as I call them, bullies? Have you ever noticed how the word bullies has the words bull (as in shit) and lies in it? Doctors = bullshit liars, basically. Psychiatrists especially.

In conclusion, the sex tape business is like any other. Fame doesn't come lightly. It's about hard work and stick-to-itiveness. It's out there—42 seconds of tantalizing erotic spectacle cast adrift on the great Klondike River of the internet. Won't you haul it aboard the Alaska-bound cruise ship, or even hijacked Somali pirate vessel, of your hard-drive? Please? You don't even have to watch it. Just download the thing, please. Please download it, you assholes, please.

Why You Beasting?

David Don Miller

> Play
> Male
> 46
> Comic

Mr. Michael Schwartz, a beleaguered math teacher in an urban high school, bursts into the teacher's lounge to vent about his unruly students. He speaks rapid-fire and nonstop.

MR. SCHWARTZ:

I really don't know what it is they expect us to teach these people when when when when when when when there's no accountability. If these people don't wanna learn, it's not going to do much good if we don't have any support. The system is designed so that the wheels just keep turning, keep turning, keep turning but but but but what are they turning out? Certainly not well-educated people—not respectful people, not people in possession of the skills necessary to succeed in corporate America. Of course the system wants everyone to get caught in the bottleneck to the same destination: college and corporate America. But how are these people supposed to compete in that world if they can't even do long division? When when when when when when when I ask a question and the response is "suck a dick," I don't know how someone could even balance a checkbook without simple math, simple long division—but that hardly matters because there's no accountability. There's no accountability on top, so there's no accountability anywhere. These people aren't here to learn, they don't know my name, they don't care what I'm teaching. They are only learning math skills at all because they spend all of their energy in my classroom buying and selling candy—probably drugs along with the candy. That seems to be all they care about, that is aside from beer and sex—video games and beer and sex. I I I I I I guess I can't get through to 'em without video games and beer and sex.

You Don't Love Limbo Like I Love Limbo
Patrick McKay

> Online magazine post
> Male
> 20s-40s
> Comic

Yep. Time to bring the limbo dance craze back. And this is just the guy to do it.

LIMBO GUY:

You don't love limbo like I love limbo. You just don't. You can't aspire to such passionate limbo heights. You can't match my sociopathic embrace of limbo culture. You can't compete with my misguided limbo devotion. Or comprehend the depths I've plunged to advance my limbo craft, the great sacrifices I've made—like eliminating all non-limbo conversation with other living beings. And sex.

I've practiced limbo since before you were a Tiki sparkle in your daddy's Mai Tai. I've forgotten more about limbo than you'll ever learn at your limbo-themed swinger parties. I've witnessed more in the limbo trenches then you've had written out for you in your Princess Cruises program guide. Fact is, I love limbo like a coconut oil motorcade and you barely know how to spell the word. L-I-M-B-O. It's not even hard. (…)

Just for the sake of argument, let's assume you might love limbo. Let's give you the benefit of the ol' limbo doubt. Then why don't you have Chubby Checker's "Limbo Rock" on continuous loop through the built-in speakers in your recently-plundered-by-divorce, furniture-less home? Need I ask more?

Here's a quick one. Why haven't you converted your basement into a Jamaican steel-pan shanty with two separate bamboo racks with peg sets every six inches?

Trick question! Limbo is not from Jamaica! It's from Trinidad! Land of hummingbirds and limbo! The real question is, why doesn't your basement feel like a Gulf-of-Paria Coquette sanctuary with three limbo racks made from the native Açaí palm and peg sets every two inches, motherfucker!?

You're Invited!
Darren Canady

> Play
> Male
> 20s-30s
> Comic

Paul just wants a little nice up in here.

PAUL:

And what is so wrong with being nice? What is so wrong with a few nice people getting together, eating some damn cake, and pretending for just a few hours that they actually enjoy each other's company? I don't think it's asking too much for people to put on a happy fucking face, haul out some manners and good breeding, and do it all in the name of a four-year-old having a happy goddamned birthday. Pretend, dammit! Nice people do it all the time. I'm nice—I do it! I pretend that I want you here, in my house, choking down my four-hundred-dollar cake and guzzling down the summer punch I made from mint leaves from my own garden. Because that's what nice queers do! We invite the half-Jew, half-black family and the anti-social single mom to the party because there ought be some goddamned solidarity even if you're all raging jackasses and vicious bitches, which I can't tell you, you are, because I'm the nice one, and could a few other people please join me in being fucking nice?!

FEMALE
SERIOCOMIC MONOLOGUES

All's Well That Ends Well
William Shakespeare

> Play
> Female
> 25+
> Seriocomic

Helena confesses that she's not upset about her father's death, but about the departure of Bertram, upon whom she has a serious crush.

HELENA:

O, were that all! I think not on my father;
And these great tears grace his remembrance more
Than those I shed for him. What was he like?
I have forgot him: my imagination
Carries no favour in't but Bertram's.
I am undone: there is no living, none,
If Bertram be away. 'Twere all one
That I should love a bright particular star
And think to wed it, he is so above me:
In his bright radiance and collateral light
Must I be comforted, not in his sphere.
The ambition in my love thus plagues itself:
The hind that would be mated by the lion
Must die for love. 'Twas pretty, though plague,
To see him every hour; to sit and draw
His arched brows, his hawking eye, his curls,
In our heart's table; heart too capable
Of every line and trick of his sweet favour:
But now he's gone, and my idolatrous fancy
Must sanctify his reliques. Who comes here?

Annie Jump

Reina Hardy

> Play
> Female
> 13
> Seriocomic

Annie, a 13-year old science genius, interrupts KJ's explanation of nucleosynthesis. KJ is a 14-year old computer geek who played a prank on Annie's father.

ANNIE:

JUST PLEASE STOP TALKING.

First of all, stop screwing up the curve of binding energy.

Second of all, why do you think your crappy explanation of nucleosynthesis is going to impress me? Why do you think you can use science I already know as a pickup line?

And even if that did impress me, which it doesn't, and even if you were cute, which you're not, you are not a good person. You are being really, really, really mean. To my father. Not to some rando, but to my dad. And it wasn't even your idea. You're weak. You're a follower, and you've got no freakin' empathy.

And let me tell you something about Dr. Alien, ok? He might be crazy, but he's not a cynic. He's willing to believe in something bigger than himself. And that makes him closer to greatness than you.

You. Will. Never. Be. Anything. Kenneth Jerome Urbanik.

So why don't you run to your little friends, and come up with more little schemes to make Peter Stockholm giggle. I have real work.

Bachelorette
Leslye Headland

> Play
> Female
> Teen
> Seriocomic

Katie, a recent prom queen, is partying in a posh hotel room while her friends snort coke. Their friend, absent from this gathering, is getting married in the morning, and this sends Katie into paroxysms of jealousy and self-loathing.

KATIE:

I just hope I'm married by thirty. If I'm not married by thirty, I will kill myself. I know you think I'm kidding but I'm not. I'll fucking put the barrel of a shotgun in my mouth.

I'm totally calm. I just don't want to be thirty and still working in retail and NOT married. I'll fucking kill myself. I'll be like a bunion on the foot of the human race. I mean you're complaining about Frank but at least you have those retarded kids to save. You're interesting. You have a noble, like, crusade at the hospital and... And at least you have a guy. At least you're getting cock. I don't even have prospective cock to passive-aggressively manipulate into marrying me.

Connected
Lia Romeo

> Play
> Female
> 30s
> Seriocomic

As she helps her daughter, Meghan, get ready for prom, Jerralyn tells her own prom story.

JERRALYN:

Did I ever tell you about the first time I went to prom? (…) This senior, this boy who was on the track team, he asked me. I hardly knew him, but it was exciting, so I said sure, I'd go. He drove this ancient pickup truck, like you could actually see the road through the holes in the floor bed, and when he showed up in this thing I thought oh, God…but I had my sparkly blue dress and my pumps and it wasn't like I could back out now, so off we went. And halfway there the car starts making this awful sputtering noise, and then stops, stops dead. So he's got his head under the hood in his suit jacket, and he says it broke a belt and he can't fix it, he'll have to come back for it tomorrow. So we start walking. And then the heel of my shoe breaks, just snaps right off, and I'm like listen, let's just…But he picks me up and carries me the rest of the way there. (…)

We were over an hour late, but we got to the dance. *(Beat.)* And then his ex-girlfriend was there, and she was this beautiful dark-haired girl in a tight red dress, very sophisticated…and he asked if I'd mind if he had one dance with her…and then they spent the rest of the night sticking their tongues down each other's throats. And none of my friends were there, since I was a freshman, so I spent the night barefoot, sitting by myself next to the punch table watching other people dance. (…)

(Beat.)

You know, I wasn't [sad.] I figured I was at prom, and that was worth something…and besides I'd had an adventure. It wasn't 'til I got a little older than I figured out that experiencing things wasn't necessarily the same as enjoying them. (…)

You're going to have an amazing time, Meggie.

Dissonance
Craig Pospisil

> Play
> Female
> Early 30s
> Seriocomic

Tricia shares her reaction upon hearing of her mother's death, after a long, terrible sickness.

TRICIA:

I was at LAX just about ready to board a plane when they called to tell me she died. I was too stunned to do anything but just get on the plane to come home.

I got bumped up to first class. Isn't that something? I travel a lot for work, and I'd just gotten enough frequent flyer miles to make the Silver Medallion class of membership. And I got upgraded. It was like they knew. I sit down and they give me a hot towel, which I press to my face, let the warmth sink into my skin. Then they bring me a mimosa. And when I finish that…they bring another. And a third. Then somewhere over Nebraska…I snap. And I get up in the aisle and start tearing my clothes off, telling everyone on the plane what a terrible daughter I am because my mother who I haven't seen in five months just died alone. (…) I was almost totally naked before a flight attendant wrapped one of those pathetic little blankets around me while I was trying to unhook my bra. They got me back to my seat, and then several passengers offered up Xanax…so the rest of the trip was pretty calm.

Drive Thru
Mark Harvey Levine

> Play
> Female
> 18-30
> Seriocomic

Bess is working the window at a drive-thru fast food restaurant.
A lonely guy in the line has tried to engage her in conversation.

BESS:

This is a fast food restaurant, sir. Fast. Food.

You can't even find *regular* nutrition here, sir, let alone something for your soul. Why is it that everyone who wakes up lonely at two in the morning decides to come here? Where does it say "Reassurance" on the menu? On any menu? You want a conversation, pal? You want to reach out? There are millions of hungry people out there—and not just hungry for attention, they're hungry for actual food. You know them, they're the ones you drive by every day. Why don't you take one of them out to dinner some night? I dare you to look them in the eye! You'll have some human contact all right. You'll have conversation. More than you can stand. And if you can't do that, then do something else! There's millions of things that need doing in this world! Do one of them! Now order some damn food so I don't lose my job.

Elephant
Margie Stokley

>Play
>Female
>17
>Seriocomic

Michelle, 17, addresses a therapy group for the first time.

MICHELLE:

Hi. My name is Michelle (*She does an 'I'm crazy' gesture and noise that somehow mocks suicide.*) Just kidding. No, really—thrilled to be here. What do you want to know? What do you want me to say...

(Silence.)

Oh, wait, that's right. This is not a conversation—it's a session. This is my time to share, with complete strangers how I feel... Well, I feel like talking about trees. How do you feel about them? Wait. Please, don't speak...let me. My fascination *stems* from this one tree. *(She silently mouths "stems" again to emphasize the irony.)* Rough crowd. *(A pause.)* Well, it's gigantic and right outside my bedroom window. Some nights I feel like it wants in. Wants in to my perfect pink-and-white-striped room. My room is perfect, not because it's everything I want. It's just perfectly planned, the pillows, the balloon shades, the pictures, the bed, the window seat, my stuffed animals. I have even more animals under my bed. I have guilt about suffocating them...I feel...it doesn't matter. They don't match. *(A pause.)* They really don't. Well, it can't fall now because I just predicted it. What you think is going to happen—never does. It's a relief. You can't know it all. I just feel like in *my movie* that that's what will happen. There'll be huge thunderstorm with lightning, my tree will explode, and I'll be crushed. I can see myself split in half. I don't want to be surrounded by all those people who would need to be there if I got crushed. I am over groups. No offense.

Flesh and the Desert

Carson Kreitzer

> Play
> Female
> 30s-40s
> Seriocomic

Josie, a Las Vegas showgirl, is interviewed in her backstage dressing room.

JOSIE:

Soon there will be no glamour left.

One night I'm standing up there, in the dark. In my five
thousand dollar Bob Mackie gown. It's topless, but it's still
a gown. This gorgeous draped blue velvet, with rhinestones
on it like stars.

The lights hit me and I hear this guy out in the audience
this guy comin' through from Bumfuck, Idaho or godknows
where clear as day he says

She looks just like Venus.

Now, you don't get that dancin' on a pole.

Men don't think you look like the ancient Greek goddess
of Love.

> *(Listens.)*

Really? It's Roman? Who's the Greek—

never mind.

Anyway, you don't look like the goddess of anything,
hangin' off a pole.

You look like, excuse me, but you look like you need the
money.

Now don't get me wrong. We all need the money. That's
why we're here.

But standing up under those lights
in a blue velvet gown with stars on it send little beams of
light shooting around the gallery when you walk?

You don't feel

like you need the money not when you're up there.

You feel like maybe maybe

You're a Goddess

if their feet hurt, too.

Full Plate Collection

Irene Ziegler

> Play
> Female
> Teen
> Seriocomic

Rosie the Riveter's teenaged daughter, who dresses like General Patton, gives her mother what-for when she learns Rosie wants to quit her job at the munitions factory.

THE GENERAL:

Now mother, what in the Sam Hill is all this nonsense about you quitting your job at the aircraft factory?

I shouldn't have to tell you there's work to be done. A stay-at-home mother is bad for morale. Our men need to know that We Can Do It!

All this stuff going around about women not wanting to work is a lot of Dippity Doo. Real women love the heat of a stinking sweatshop. That aircraft factory is hiring the best women this century has seen. Yes, you're going to have to make sacrifices. You'll have to trade your open-toed pumps for steel toe boots, but by golly, you're going to wear them, and look good in them, too!

You know something, mother? By the time this war is over, nineteen thousand women will have entered the workforce. I pity the men who will take over those jobs once they come back home. Leapin' lizards, I do, because women are going to raise the bar so high, then men will wish they had been born with ovaries, too.

Now, you may be worried that once your factory job is over, you may not remember how to care for your family. Don't worry about that. After one week back at home, you'll be crying over the stove just like you never left. And seventy years from now, when you're sitting around the TV with your great-granddaughter sitting on your bladder, and she asks what you did in the great war, you won't have to say, "Climb down, honey. Gramma needs to wee."

All right, mother, you know how I feel. The decision is yours to make. Oh, one more thing. No matter what you decide, I will be proud to be your daughter, not just because you're my mother, but because I *see* you, and I think you're pretty amazing.

That's all.

Good Luck

Katy Wix

> Freestanding monologue
> Female
> 30s-40s
> Seriocomic

This British woman worries just a bit.

WOMAN:

(…) I worry about so much.

I worry about the ice-caps melting. My thighs. My eyebrows. I'm always irked. But I cannot stand, I cannot stand, I cannot stand, I cannot stand, I cannot stand seeing other girls being insecure. I just want to shake them and tell them what a huge waste of energy it is. I mean, right now for example, I'm worried about what I'm going to eat today because I've had breakfast but nothing since. I'm worried about a comment that I wrote on Facebook earlier that no one has liked yet—it wasn't funny enough and I should delete it. I worry that I'm going to fall and break all my teeth, which is stupid I know, or that the world might end really suddenly. I have nightmares about that one. Sometimes it's an asteroid, which isn't a million miles away from reality, well it is a million miles away, actually, well, light years rather than miles but, still, could happen. Or another volcano.

I worry that there's probably a hundred ways to wear a scarf and I only know about four of them. I worry that I'll drop my phone into water every time I'm near some water. I worry about that all the time. I worry that I spend way too much time practising that I'm on a chat show.

I guess the headline is: I'm a lot of fun, clearly. Five minutes spent with me and you will either feel much better about your own life or you will, like me, disappear down a rabbit hole of existential angst. Good luck.

I am Your Waitress
Kate Sederstrom

Essay
Female
20s-40s
Seriocomic

This waitress says what food servers think.

WAITRESS:

Welcome! My name is Kate and I'll be helping y'all out this evening. Can I get you started with anything to drink? I am your waitress, with a bright smile etched on my face as I jot down your drink orders and say with the syrupy sweet high-pitched voice, "Of course!" "Not a problem!" and "My pleasure!"

I memorize tonight's specials so you don't have to read them; I'm happy to explain every menu item in excruciating detail; I'll make sure to tell the chef not to overcook your salmon, apologize profusely when it comes to your table slightly less moist than you prefer, then offer you a new one in addition to the free dessert.

I drop the check to the oldest man at the table and thank your party for coming out this evening and for being such a pleasure.

By the way, in case you were wondering, I do create the recipes for the food you don't like, I personally delay the dish that comes out just a little too late, and I created the policy that we don't sell half quesadillas. I find your condescending jokes genuinely amusing and I am too deaf to hear the snide remarks you make about me within earshot: "I'm surprised she's still working here after last week's service."

I am your waitress, who, with a furrowed brow, apologizes when you get croutons on your salad — when, by God, you're gluten free. No, it's not Celiac disease, but you feel so much better without gluten in your diet. My only purpose is to delight you. My permanent address is the employee break room, where I live without family, friends, or a future. I live to serve.

I Think You Think I Love You

Kelly Younger

> Play
> Female
> 26-40
> Seriocomic

Branwyn relates the rather unfortunate memorial service she conducted for her mother.

BRANWYN:

I take out mom's ashes. I recite a line from Shakespeare—*Othello*, she liked that play. Actually, no. I don't think she ever saw it. Or even read it. God what am I talking about? I've never read it. I searched and searched for the perfect poem or song or quotation or something to say at that moment, but I couldn't find anything, so I flipped open a book of Shakespeare plays—he's supposed to be the best, right?—and just dropped my finger down into a play and it was *Othello* so that's what I memorized and that's what I said. And then I said…goodbye mom…and tossed her ashes up in the air. And by air, of course, I mean wind, and by *wind*, I mean the wind blowing in the direction I'm standing and I'm sorry, but I never paid much attention to those old sailor movies that say never spit into the wind, because sure enough mom blows right out and back at me. And by back at me, of course, I mean my face and by my face I mean my nose and mouth. So of course my face is all wet and weepy so mom sticks to my face, and I freak out and inhale with horror and down she goes. Not all of it, or her, but enough, you know? Just a bit to be absolutely horrified that I've just inhaled some of my mother, which I'm sure could be some beautiful metaphor for mom living inside me and all that sentimental bull, but really all I can think is my mother tastes like charcoal. Not that I know, but you can imagine, you know? So I start pouring water out of my canteen onto my face and into my mouth and nose and I'm stumbling all around the top of Castle Rock thinking I'm either going straight to hell for cannibalizing my mother or I'm going straight off the side of this rock like that old Indian girl who couldn't live without her lover. It's okay, you can laugh.

Jenny's Gigantic Freak-Out

Nina Louise Morrison

> Freestanding monologue
> Female
> 22
> Seriocomic

Jenny, a klutzy but energetic sex-ed teacher, has a paranoid panic-tantrum-breakdown over what she might say to her boyfriend and his best friend, who she secretly fears are having an affair.

JENNY:

Maybe you've been sleeping with each other all along,
maybe you've been meeting in secret in the city,
that one time he didn't call me for like two days,
he was fucking you and making art and drinking and smoking pot and buying kitschy things for your apartment and the whole time I'm sitting here like an asshole teaching a bunch of assholes where their asshole is and why they shouldn't use it until they have a *committed partner* when what the fuck does that mean?

I could have slept with Jordan Fleishman that time he came on to me so hard at that Christmas party, I could have pushed him into the bathroom and fucked him right there with you lighting fireworks on the pond out back,

but *no* you told me you *loved me* and you were *ready* and *it's never been like this with anyone.*

Well, you didn't say it like that,
but you *said some stuff*
and you *did some stuff*
and I *believed* it like the sucker I am and it's just not *fair*!

Where was *she* where was she when you thought you swallowed a hornet, huh? Who sat with you in the emergency room and held your hand and listened to you freak out for 4 hours and talked you down when you thought your throat was going to swell up so much you couldn't breathe?

She was in New York with her *girlfriend* because she's a *lesbian* so snap out of it!

Lost Love, The Final 100 Years #5
Peter Papadopoulos

> Play
> Female
> 20s-30s
> Seriocomic

Jan seeks to escape the pain of her partner Barb's infidelity by quitting her job and dropping out of civilized life. Here she describes to Barb what will happen now that they can no longer afford to pay their bills.

JAN:

First they'll turn off the power,
and then I'll just lie in bed in the dark
and stare at the blank TV
while I wait for the people from the bank to come
to take the house,
and move me and the furniture out into the street,
still sitting in my bed
out in the street
in my favorite blue and green PJs.
right where they cart me out and drop me,
the bank people, in their suits and ties,
all official like
and then I'll just sit there
in my PJs
in my bed
and wait.
And what will happen next?
It's probably not the bank people who come, huh?
I bet they hire somebody.
Some crew or something.
Big angly guys with scruffy faces and hard, squinty eyes
and big bulges on the sides of their waistbands
where they conceal their illegal hand guns.
But they're not bad guys after all
not deep down
    they just had a tough life
    and ended up stuck here somehow

in this stinky town
in this stinky job
and they need this job right now
so they can eat
and pay their child support
and buy lotto tickets
and so they must do their job
this job
moving me out into the street.
I don't resent them for it.
They look at me
with a sort of
curious compassion
strained through their guarded, steely eyes
—compassionate, yes—
but unflinching,
as they carry me out
bed and all
into the street.
And who can blame them?
These mover guys.
And although they feel for me
they don't really know me,
and they've become accustomed to this,
all in a day's work
blocking it out
holding it down
whatever feelings they might have left
because, it is, after all,
just their job.
And when they set me down in the street
the bed hits the pavement with a
crunchy, metallic pop.
I shake for just a moment,
and then
stillness.
And I'm sitting in my bed in the middle of the street
surrounded by all this stuff.
Sofas and lamps and laptops and bookcases and toasters and iron-
ing boards.

And after a few moments
I look over towards the house
what used to be our house
and I see
these official-looking people standing outside
—THESE must be the bank people—
and they are just finishing changing the locks.
And they look over at me and call out
"GOOD LUCK!"

Measure for Measure
William Shakespeare

> Play
> Female
> 25+
> Seriocomic

In Isabella's book, men who try to play God are like apes trying to be men. Makes sense.

ISABELLA:
Could great men thunder
As Jove himself does, Jove would ne'er be quiet,
For every pelting, petty officer
Would use his heaven for thunder;
Nothing but thunder! Merciful Heaven,
Thou rather with thy sharp and sulphurous bolt
Split'st the unwedgeable and gnarled oak
Than the soft myrtle: but man, proud man,
Drest in a little brief authority,
Most ignorant of what he's most assured,
His glassy essence, like an angry ape,
Plays such fantastic tricks before high heaven
As make the angels weep; who, with our spleens,
Would all themselves laugh mortal.

The Money Shot
Neil LaBute

> Play
> Female
> 30s
> Seriocomic

Karen, a movie star, has invited her co-star and his wife to dinner at her Hollywood mansion, and is distracted by the sounds of traffic.

KAREN:

OH MY GOD! THAT SOUND! DRIVES ME CRAZY! Can you hear it... hear that?!

(Holds up her hand, signaling to MISSY and STEVE.)

God, look at 'em down there!! All those fucking cars on the 101! I hate traffic! That's the one thing about this town—I love my work and the, you know, *fans* and all that, but—the roads are shit!! They really are. You pay so much for a home...nice home in the hills and people come to a goddamn stand-still, right in front of our gate...right there! It's insane! Police sirens all the time and those...like, *emergency* vehicles...and you know what? It's gotten to the point where I just started cheering 'em on! No, I do! If I hear a wreck or people sitting on their horns, I'll come out here and I'll just start screaming, YES! YES! YES!! I mean, if I gotta listen to this all the time, then I want blood and fire...know what I'm saying? I don't want a goddamn *Subaru* in the diamond lane with a flat tire! No, fuck that! I want bodies and death and, like, *chaos*!! That's what I want!!

(Looking at STEVE and MISSY.)

It's a nice view, though, otherwise. From up here...

A Mother's Love
Craig Pospisil

> Freestanding Monologue
> Female
> 30s-40s
> Seriocomic

Melissa enters wearing a conservative suit. She smiles warmly at the audience.

MELISSA:

I love my husband. Even now, I still love Kevin. Now, he thought it was time to send Theresa to school, and I know he had his reasons. School can be a valuable experience. (*Slight pause.*) But times change. School isn't the same as it was when we were children. My first day of school I was so scared about being separated from my parents and about being surrounded by kids I didn't know. Imagine how much more frightening that would be today, knowing that many of your classmates were A– R – M– E– D? (*Slight pause.*) Now, look, I'm not saying anything would happen while she was in kindergarten…of course not. (*Slight pause.*) But after that who knows? (*Slight pause.*) Will Teresa make it to third grade before she starts doing D – R– U– G– S at recess? And after D – R – U– G– S, how long will it take before she's drawn into a world of S– E – X? And S– E– X and D – R– U– G– S lead right to P-R-O-S-T-I-T-U-T-I-O-N. (*Slight pause.*) Did I spell that right? Let me see P-R-O… well, I mean she could become a H-O-O-K-E-R. (*Pause.*) Not my little girl. (*Pause.*) I tried to convince Kevin we should keep Theresa at home and teach her ourselves. He didn't understand, and we got into a big F-I-G-H-T. I try to talk about it in a calm, reasonable way, but Kevin lost his T-E-M-P-E-R and Y-E-L-L-E-D, and that made Theresa cry. I couldn't have let that happen. (*Slight pause.*) Ladies and gentlemen of the jury… Yes, I K-I-L-L-E-D my husband. But what I did was a form of self-defense. I was protecting my daughter the way any of you would. Theresa is too young to see the world for what it is. She needs to be protected. And that is why I am innocent of M-U-R-D-E-R. (*Pause.*) Thank you.

Out of the Water
Brooke Berman

> Play
> Female
> 17
> Seriocomic

Cat is by herself on a train to New York City. She speaks to fellow travelers.

CAT:

I work very hard. I get A's in all of my classes. I am on time for everything. For Everything. I work harder than the boys but I don't get rewarded. I hear there was this thing a long time ago called "The Revolution" but my mom doesn't seem to know about it. My mom is always exhausted. Church doesn't help. My mom is on a lot of committees and medication. I think my mom wants my dad to come home. My dad went to see his ex-stepsister in New York and he never came back. I don't know what he's doing there. I mean, ex-stepsister? That's not even a real relation. Plus, she's like, she's not, you know, she's not a Christian. I think she must lead a very scandalous and potentially exciting life even if it does not fall under the contract or rubric or whatever of the Church of God. I went on the Internet this morning and looked up this Polly Freed. I know a lot about her. I am going to get my father back. I am going to bring him home. Mom's in the bedroom with the lights out again and everything's quiet and sometimes, you just have to take matters into your own hands. Do you know what I mean?

The Potato Creek Chair of Death
Robert Kerr

> Play
> Female
> 20s
> Seriocomic

Linda, a waitress at a highway diner, tells her story to Cedric, who is passing through.

LINDA:

...and that's what I do. I go someplace, wait tables for a couple months, long enough to save up for a junker car. I drive it until it falls apart and wherever I end up is where I live for the next couple months. I guess maybe someday I'll settle down, but not just yet. I really get off on coming to a new town where nobody knows me: I could be anyone. It's like I can pour myself into the corners of my being I never knew were there. You spend too much time with someone and they expect you to act a certain way. Like Jeff, the cook here. I'm staying with him now, you know, and this morning we woke up and he said, "Why didn't you kiss me on the cheek? You kiss me on the cheek every morning." So now I know it's about time to move on. Five thirty-five with tax.

The Profession
Walter Wykes

> Play
> Female
> 20s-30s
> Seriocomic

A serious young woman chronicles life with a philanderer.

ROSETTA:

My husband is very experienced. He's been with hundreds of women. Thousands. On our wedding day alone, he impregnated seven bridesmaids, two caterers, the photographer, the photographer's assistant, her youngest daughter, the preacher's wife, my third-grade English teacher, a marine biologist, two blue whales, and one old woman who just happened to wander in off the street. He has no morals, you see. He thinks they're very old fashioned. He's a philosopher! But he liked the idea of having a virgin, you know, tarnishing the flower, plucking the petal, all that—it was very exciting for him. Unfortunately, he knew, being a philosopher, that the moment he actually did it, everything would be ruined. So as soon as the ceremony was over, he locked me away in a little room with his galoshes. In addition, he had a problem with his feet. A certain...odor...and the galoshes...well... you know. I used to beg him to release me. To have his way. Or at least put a bullet through my head. But he wouldn't do it. Except on Sundays. On Sundays, he often let me out, and we would pretend to be very happy.

The Trash Bag Tourist
Samuel Brett Williams

> Play
> Female
> 30
> Seriocomic

Molly, a rodeo clown with a dream, lives with her dilapidated mother in a dilapidated trailer in Arkadelphia, Arkansas, a dilapidated town. She talks to Chuck, a "trash bag tourist," which is a reference to hurricane Katrina refugees.

MOLLY:

Ya' ain't never been to a rodeo? (…) I'm a rodeo clown. (…) Meanin' I distract the bulls. Keep 'em from sitting on riders and stuff. (…) Everyone works a rodeo is always hurt—ya' just don't wanna get injured—that means you can't do it no more. Bull got its horns in my barrel once and cracked my nose. Iced it 'tween rides. Next day—I didn't have ta wear no clown paint. My eyes wuz as black as a farmer's mornin' coffee. (…)

When I'm out there, and the rider's been bucked—I can feel everyone's eyes—in a good way. They're watchin' with hope—hope that I'm gonna keep the bull from gettin' the rider—hope that I'm gonna keep the bull from gettin' me. That bull—he's death—and I'm dancin' with him. I can smell his sweat, and he can smell mine. We respect each other.

(Beat. Pointing to the bookshelf.)

That belt—it's got real gold in it. Most valuable thing I own. Arkadelphia Rodeo Association gave it to me for my "heroism in the line of fire." (…) It actually has Brandon Smith's name on it, but a bull tore off his face 'fore they could give it to him, so they gave it to me instead. (…) Tomorrow I got a tryout for the PRCA Tour. It goes all across the South. If they pick me up as a professional rodeo clown, then I'll be rich. We're talkin' like four hundred dollars a week. Plus vacation.

The Two Gentlemen of Verona
William Shakespeare

> Play
> Female
> 16-20
> Seriocomic

Julia, a young woman in love, has received a love letter from Proteus and in a fit of pique, tears it up before having read it. Here, the impetuous young woman gathers all the scraps and tries to piece the letter back together again.

JULIA:

Nay, would I were so anger'd with the same!
O hateful hands, to tear such loving words!
Injurious wasps, to feed on such sweet honey
And kill the bees that yield it with your stings!
I'll kiss each several paper for amends.
Look, here is writ 'kind Julia.' Unkind Julia!
As in revenge of thy ingratitude,
I throw thy name against the bruising stones,
Trampling contemptuously on thy disdain.
And here is writ 'love-wounded Proteus.'
Poor wounded name! my bosom as a bed
Shall lodge thee till thy wound be thoroughly heal'd;
And thus I search it with a sovereign kiss.
But twice or thrice was 'Proteus' written down.
Be calm, good wind, blow not a word away
Till I have found each letter in the letter,
Except mine own name: that some whirlwind bear
Unto a ragged fearful-hanging rock
And throw it thence into the raging sea!
Lo, here in one line is his name twice writ,
'Poor forlorn Proteus, passionate Proteus,
To the sweet Julia:' that I'll tear away.
And yet I will not, sith so prettily
He couples it to his complaining names.
Thus will I fold them one on another:
Now kiss, embrace, contend, do what you will.

When in Rome
Ben Verschoor

Freestanding monologue
Female
20+
Seriocomic

A Latin teacher toasts the end of her career.

TEACHER:

"Why Latin?" I think you mean, "*Quare Latinam?*"

Why teach Latin? To answer that, I turn to the Myth of Sisyphus. I trust you all know of Sisyphus? Sisyphus, I would remind you, was condemned to roll a boulder up a hill, every day, for all eternity. His triumph, according to the French, is the realization of the pointlessness of his ask, and his momentary relief when he walks back down the hill before doing it all over again.

Sounds bad, but I ask you: what if Sisyphus had actually come to enjoy pushing the boulder? What if he had made peace with his situation, and stopped looking for meaning and satisfaction in the outcome, and instead found it in the process and the moment? What then, would Sisyphus do if he learned that because of budget cuts there would be no more boulder next semester? He wouldn't be Sisyphus anymore. *(Silence.)*

So you know what, fuck Sisyphus. Fuck Sisyphus, fuck the Greeks, fuck the French too. When…Cato, when Cato the Younger, the *Roman* statesman, learned the war against Julius Caesar was lost, he didn't cry or beg for mercy. He disemboweled himself, literally ripped his own guts out, because he would rather die than suffer the indignity of living under Caesar. Cato kept it real.

(Reaches into a handbag and pulls out... a wine bottle.) If I'm going to be fired, I want it to be for a good reason. A good vintage. *(Examines bottle.)* "*In vino veritas.*" "In wine, there is truth." You don't need a semester of high school Latin to know that. You go to enough bars and bistros, and it becomes a refrain. *(Opens bottle.)* Also a convenient excuse. Cheers, class. "Si fueris Rōmae, Rōmānō vīvitō more."

"When in Rome, do as the Romans do."

Where's Julie?

Daniel Guyton

> Play
> Female
> 15
> Seriocomic

Julie is a young girl who is pregnant and very confused. Her friend Margaret convinces her to pray to Jesus for answers. Unfortunately, Julie has never been the "praying" type...

JULIE:

Dear Jesus, I'm sorry I called you a crock of shit. I just...
(She drops her hands onto the bed.)
    I'm not very good at this. Praying. Talking to someone who isn't there. Or maybe you *are* there, Jesus. I don't know. But it sure doesn't seem like you care anymore. Is that what it is? You're there, but you just don't care anymore? Because that seems more likely if you ask me.
    (Pause.) Not that I blame you, Jesus. I wouldn't care either if I was you. Here you are, dying for everybody's sins, and yet... here we all are—still sinning. People are terrible, aren't we Jesus? Allowing you to die like that? All alone...*(Pause)* So here's the question of the hour, Mr. Jesus. Should I have this baby? Because wouldn't it be a *bigger* sin to bring him into a world like this? Full of pain and...loneliness? And what if I have this baby, and he doesn't love me? What if he turns on me, the way we...well, the way most of us...have turned on you? *(Pause.)* I think I know how You felt now, Jesus. On the cross. Alone. Sacrificing *everything* for someone else. For everyone.
    Are you there? Jesus?

Whore: A Kid's Play
Reese Thompson

> Play
> Female
> Teen
> Seriocomic

Jenn wants two things from God: 1) to be pretty, and 2) for Andrea to be her BFF.

JENN:

Dear God. Um, so.... How are you? *(Eye-roll and a sigh.)*

Ok, look. I know my parents are secular humanists and technically I'm not even *supposed* to be talking to you, but I figure if God *did* exist, He wouldn't be a petty li'l bitch about it is all I'm saying? I know what you're thinking: I haven't decided whether you exist or not either. I can see how that could be a problem! But you know, all that could change based on how this works out.

(A beat.)

You can probably tell I've never done this before. Like, are there forms I'm supposed to fill out? Should we discuss terms of service? And say my prayers aren't answered in a timely manner, is there a complaints department I can call? I tried searching google, but... I guess this is gonna have to count as my first act of faith. Besides, I figure you couldn't have stayed in business this long if customer satisfaction weren't at least... above average. *(...)*

Anyway, I wouldn't bother you if this weren't *extremely* important!

(A beat.)

God? Please make me pretty. No. Scratch that. Please make me really *really* hot! Like Julia Roberts, but when she was young and people liked her. And I swear I'm not being conceited! This is about justice! And quality of life! And—! And what if Andrea hears someone call me "hairy Mary" or "shit-stains" and decides I'm not cool enough to hang out with? And maybe I'm not cool enough, but she doesn't have to know that! I'm not asking for much here. Just one friend to make this sucky existence a little more bearable!

(Beat.)

And not to place blame on anyone, but if you were a JUST

God.... See where I'm going with this? So... to recap: please make me hot. And please make Andrea agree to be my best friend. Amen... or... whatever.

A Woman and a Pen
Angel Propps

> Freestanding monologue
> Female
> 26-40
> Seriocomic

Sitting at a bar, Clarissa is talking to another woman while a bartender cleans glasses.

CLARISSA:

So I got the divorce papers today. I opened them up and there they were—all neat and folded and stapled and signed. Little red tabs on the pages where I'm to sign. I wanted to sign, I really did, but I couldn't find a single ink pen in the whole house. The whole house! How can I not have a pen? And why do divorce papers not come through email or some online document signing service? I mean really? In today's world when everyone has tablets and computers and…

(Pauses to take a drink.)

I couldn't find an ink pen. I couldn't believe it. I mean that idiot cheated on me with every woman who got within a twenty-mile radius of him and I thought, I really thought I took everything, and boy did he deserve to be kicked to the curb with nothing but one suitcase and his car keys, but he somehow managed to abscond with every single stupid pen in the whole house! I wanted to sign. I mean there it was, right there in my hands, freedom! Only it had to be signed for and he must have taken the ink pens just to spite me.

(Shakes her head and takes another drink.)

I was desperate. I was ready to open a vein and sign in blood if that was what it took. Then I thought maybe, just maybe, that is what he wants. My blood on the page I mean. So I went out to get a pen and I ended up here. I don't know how or why I wound up here either. I don't even know why I'm talking about this. Hey, bartender! Can I get my tab?

(Bartender comes over, slides across a small leather book holding the check. Clarissa opens it. Begins to laugh.)

Of course. There's a pen.

MALE
SERIOCOMIC MONOLOGUES

7th Period Lunch, or Someone's Gonna Snap (#2)
David Don Miller

Play
Male
18
Seriocomic

Kenny Hills is white and speaks with a self-consciously urban dialect. He is a slippery eel of a young man, with swagger for days. After his teacher, Mr. Fredericks, tells him he failed another test and that he will never amount to anything but a drain on society, Kenny confronts him.

KENNY:

Yeah well I failed my test. Again. And no disrespect, but fuck you, Mr. Fredericks. Yo. Mr. Puglese said some shit to me, called me all kinds a names. He a racist motherfucker too. But you? You worse. You're just a nasty ass bastard being a nasty ass cause you angry about su'mm. You angry at yourself for being stuck doin' a job you hate. Word. Yo I been takin' tests for deadass twelve years and every one of them tells me the same thing. What's the letter that come home say? I read that shit first to make sure my moms never sees it: *Your son*—blank space with Kenny Hill written in that shit—*is in need of academic intervention services.* What that even means? It means I need extra help, right? Yeah I get that. But why they call it an intervention? I need an intervention? I been needing an intervention for twelve years and they don't give me one? Yo. I dead watch that show "Intervention" on the regular, okay? And when they have an intervention, they surround some dude with all the people in his life, right? Corner his ass. An' so, they all take turns tellin' this fool that if he don't stop drinkin' or doin' drugs they dead gonna cut him out they life. They don't take no twelve years to do that shit! He got one day to get his shit together! You been tellin' me twelve years that I need an intervention! What kind of intervention do I get? Extra time in a extra class with you? An angry, half-ass teacher who don't wanna be there? You call that an intervention? That's a study hall with a different name. Shit. I failed the test? You failed *your* test, nigga.

The Bleak Shall Inherit the Earth
David Rakoff

>Essay
>Male
>40s
>Seriocomic

This excerpt is from the late comic's collection, "Half Empty."

DAVID:

We were so happy. It was miserable. (…)

The Internet at that point was still newish and completely uncharted territory, to me at least. (…) But I now found myself at numerous parties for start-ups, my comprehension of which extended no further than the free snacks and drinks, and the perfume of money-scented elation in the air. The workings of "new media" remained entirely murky, and I a baffled hypocrite, scarfing down another beggar's purse with crème fraiche (flecked with just enough beads of caviar to get credit), pausing in my chewing only long enough to mutter "It'll never last." It was becoming increasingly difficult to fancy myself a guilelessly astute child at the procession who points out the Emperor's nakedness as acquaintances were suddenly becoming millionaires on paper and legions of twenty-one-year-olds were securing lucrative and rewarding positions as "content providers" instead of answering phones for a living, as I had at that age. Brilliant success was all around.

So, so happy.

Ching Chong Chinaman
Lauren Yee

> Play
> Male
> 40s
> Seriocomic

Ed, a Chinese-American, instructs a guest on the intricacies of golf.

ED:

Some people say golf is a white man's sport. I say, if you're gonna have that attitude, you might as well call America a white man's country. But look at all the Chinese Americans excelling athletically. Michelle Kwan. Yao Ming. Kristi Yamaguchi. Makes you think. Now, in the business world, golf is of the utmost importance. During those games, lives are changed. Men are made. The stakes are enormous. So when you play golf, you need to be aware. Of your grip. Of your stance. And every time you tee off, you want to ask yourself some questions. Such as:

Does my swing feel natural?

Do I commit with my follow-through?

What club should I be using?

Am I hitting it at the right spot?

Did I wash my balls today?

And most importantly: can I get it in the hole? And the answer is: no. NEVER. And you can't just upgrade your equipment because it's the only club God gave you and sometimes I just want to say, "Shut up: keep your head down and spread your legs wider and maybe it'd go in for once!" *(Stops, then...)* But that's just because you always want to aim for perfection. And practice your golf swing.

Cracker (#1)

Reese Thompson

> Play
> Male
> 30s-40s
> Seriocomic

Vengeful prophet Reverend Jedidiah Jessop, appears in religious robes under a spot.

JESSOP:

I would like to talk to you all today about a time
before I was called.

Before I came to build this holy compound where once my followers and I gathered
in both peace and abject terror.

Before the responsibility fell upon me to speak God's *personal* truth
here on earth.

It was around this time that the Lord himself came before me.
As clear as I stand before you today.

Now, as some of you may know,

I was once employed at The Resorts Hotel and Casino, a place which, by any standards, could justly be called a hub of Satanism.

I had worked my way up
from calling out bingo numbers in the senior's lounge to being appointed head blackjack dealer.

It was a position that yielded much in the way of earthly rewards but virtually zero spiritual ones. For months
I sustained myself on a diet of shellfish and cocaine yet *still*
couldn't shed those last ten pounds.

In my free time I lusted after show girls. Oh yes!

Shameless women I would photograph through a perforation I had made
in the lady's bathroom wall.

It was their fault, the temptresses.

In any event, there I was, a runny-nosed compulsive masturbator, and wouldn't you know it,
there was something missing from my life.

Then one day a man came to my table. A man not unlike you or I.

He had dazzling rings on his fingers and a long silken goatee much similar to that of a wise Chinaman or an actual billy goat.

And he said to me, 'Jessop?' And I said, 'Yes?'

And he said, 'Is this where men place their faith in in the hands of the money-changers?' And I said... 'Maybe.'

Then he laid down his chips and I laid down his cards

and he said to me, 'Jessop?' And I said, 'Yes?' And he said: 'Hit me.' And so I did.

Then he grabbed me by the lapels and shook me and said: 'Ouch! Why the hell did you do that for?'

(...)

I forget my point. Oh well. Let us pray.

Lord? Grant me the fortitude

to face the coming dangers,

to stand up to the liberal Satanists and celebrity fornicators

that lead our precious youth astray. And Lord?

Grant me the hardness of heart

to do what is necessary to visit upon those little Benedict Arnolds the full force of your wrath

and glorious retribution!

Amen.

Cracker (#2)

Reese Thompson

> Play
> Male
> 30s-40s
> Seriocomic

*Rev Jedidiah Jessop, a guitar slung over his shoulder, enters under
a spot. He's dressed in corduroy slacks, a dark turtle neck, a paisley
or floral vest, a Brady Bunch perm, and big square-shaped glasses.
He begins playing a pleasant, folksy melody.*

JESSOP:

You ever turn on the TV after a long day
and it seems no matter where you look what station you turn to
it's nothing but war and bloody carnage?
Innocent folks, like you and me, dying horrifically?
Ever stop and wonder to yourself: *what's it like*
seeing through that other man's eyes?
Walking in that attractive lady's shoes?
Ever wonder why it's so darn hard for folks to get along?
(Pause for effect.)
I do. Everyday.
*(Another pause. He plays a little louder now, switching it up,
elaborating on the previous melody. He continues to speak.)*
And y'know, it's a lot like you and me
when we go through difficult times.
When the world says to us: you're not smart enough
or handsome enough. Maybe you didn't get
that internship you wanted. Maybe someone
at the office is being weird with you
and you want to ask if it's because of something you did
but you also want to avoid confrontation.
Sometimes those are the hardest things in life to go through.
I know. I go through them.
I even cry about them from time to time.
It hurts.
But we all go through tough times in life
when we think there's no one on our side no one listening.
None of us have a monopoly on human suffering.
We're all victims in one way or another.

You might even say that's what this whole evening's about:
Other people's suffering.
(A beat, switches chords again)
Now I know some of you will wanna tell me:
'But Jessop, empathy's great if you're some kinda fag
but is it enough to change the world?
Much less keep it from falling into the hands of Godless
liberals.'
But ya see. I believe it takes more than a few gun toting loners
and sexually frustrated internet trolls
to spread the word of the disenfranchised white man.
   (Short pause.)
It takes *hearts. And minds*.
We want a voice to say to the world
'We're straight white men
and we're angry
and we don't know why.'
   (Another short pause.)
That's why I want to start this evening with a song.
About what it's like. The tears of the white man.
There's a message of love in this song. A message of hope.
It's about a man I know.
A lot of folks used tell him he wasn't good enough either.
Maybe you've heard of him.
His name was Jesus. And he was a white man.

A Dill Pickle

Katherine Mansfield

> Short story
> Male
> 40s+
> Seriocomic

*Meeting in a café after a six-year hiatus, a man indirectly insults his
ex-lover and reminds her, perhaps, why they split.*

MAN:

What a marvelous listener you are. When you look at me with
those wild eyes I feel that I could tell you things that I would never
breathe to another human being. (...) Before I met you, I had never
spoken of myself to anybody. How well I remember one night, the
night that I brought you the little Christmas tree, telling you all about
my childhood. And of how I was so miserable that I ran away and
lived under a cart in our yard for two days without being discovered.
And you listened, and your eyes shone, and I felt that you had even
made the little Christmas tree listen too, as in a fairy story. (...) It
seems such ages ago. I cannot believe that it is only six years. (...) I've
often thought how I must have bored you. And now I understand
so perfectly why you wrote to me as you did—although at the time
that letter nearly finished my life. I found it again the other day,
and I couldn't help laughing as I read it. It was so clever—such a
true picture of me. (...)

Ah, no, please (...) don't go just for a moment. (...) I see so few
people to talk to nowadays, that I have turned into a sort of barbar-
ian. (...) Have I said something to hurt you?

Havin' a Good Day

Terence Duncan

> Freestanding monologue
> Male
> 50s
> Seriocomic

Terry manages to turn a good day into a routine one.

TERRY:

I feel unusually clean today. I can't quite put my finger on it, but as I was driving into work, I just felt sort of...April Fresh. I did my normal morning routine. Nothing special. Maybe it was the good night's sleep. Maybe the warm, Spring-like weather.

I don't know. I just feel fresh and more alive than usual. If I had a dog, I'd take him for a walk. If I had a cat, I'd let him jump on the counter. If I had a kid, I'd pat them on the head and say something supportive, like "Go get 'em today, Champ." I always like that name... "Champ." Champ Duncan.

Maybe I'll call my mom and tell her I love her. Wouldn't that be nice? That's what a good son would do. But then, I'm afraid she'd think that something is wrong. She'd be like... "Why did you say that? Are you sick?" I'd say, "No. I just feel extra clean today." Then, she'd say "What does that mean? What's wrong? Are you having a stroke?" She'd get all upset and confrontational and I'd spend the next ten minutes calming her down. After our call, she'd call my brother Bill and tell him to call me and find out what's wrong. She'd do the same to Craig. Craig would call me later and say, "Mom thinks that you are sick or something. You should call her." I'd say, "I did call her." Then, I'd have to call my mom again and reassure her that nothing is wrong. I was just feeling extra fresh and alive. That, of course, will set her off again. "That doesn't make any sense!!!!"

Nope.

I think I'll just enjoy my coffee and work on my budgets today.

Honky (#2)
Greg Kalleres

> Play
> Male
> 30s
> Seriocomic

Peter, white, is an account executive in a successful marketing firm. Here, he makes it obvious to his black therapist why he's in therapy.

PETER:

(Choosing words carefully) Right. Well. To say you're not racist is ignorant and ignorance is the very seed of racism. What I mean is I don't hate someone because of the color of their skin or the slant of their eye. I don't mean *"slant"* as in…my point is, I like African Americans! *(Realizing this is stupid.)* But obviously not just because they are so. I mean, I like some and I don't like some. Like I like some white people and *hate* some white people—like any race!

And I didn't mean to imply that all racists are white either. I think racism is an equal opportunity kind of thing. Hell, *you* could be a racist. (…) You can be anything you want! That's what's so great about this country! And I don't mean to say that all racists are bad people. Some are very good people! Good people who just don't know because they didn't have the money for the education. My Aunt Judy? Total racist. But you can't blame her because she grew up poor, so it doesn't really count. And she's white!

(Chuckles.) Well, of course she's white.

(Beat.) Or she might not be! I didn't mean to imply that because I'm Caucasian she has to be Caucasian. It's very possible, not knowing me or my heritage, that she could be African American. Or Chinese. Or Asian! Not that all Chinese are Asian, obviously.

> *(Long awkward pause. Peter forces a smile, trying to look comfortable.)*

Okay. Okay. I'm going to be honest here. When I walked in and saw that you were not some whitey white, stuck up, Dr. Phil yuppie, I was so relieved. I gotta tell you, I can't wait to tell you my problems and stuff. *(Pause, coming clean.)* A kid was murdered for a pair of shoes and I think it's because of a commercial I wrote.

Honky (#3)

Greg Kalleres

> Play
> Male
> 30s
> Seriocomic

> *Peter, white, is being aggressive with his black therapist, Emilia,*
> *whom he desperately wants to date. He is less successful using wit*
> *to mask his aggression and guilt.*

PETER:

Ah! What?! What is wrong with me!??!?

What more do I have to do?! Huh!? I feel for your people! Okay? The struggle? The, the plight?! I have professed my sins! Every week I come to you, contrite! And out there, all the time, in different ways! I am sorry! Okay?! I AM SORRY FOR MY PEOPLE! They suck! Whatever they did, whenever they did it, I renounce them! THEY ARE RENOUNCED! Jesus! I'm tired of paying for shit I didn't do! Slavery! Oppression! Forty acres and the Jim Croce Laws! I didn't bring you people over here!! *(Beat.)* So, I see these black kids on the subway. They look a little sketchy and I think, "Hey, maybe I should go to the other side of the train"— but no! Because then I say to myself, "Who are you to judge?! They're probably very smart educated kids! Who am I to assume that just because they're African American, they don't read Sartre?!" But guess what?! They pulled a fucking gun on me anyway! It didn't matter what I thought! So fuck them! And fuck *guilt!* I'm tired of it!! Watching my tongue, policing every syllable that comes out of my mouth! So, do me a favor, will you? Tell every black person or African American that you know that it wasn't me! Can you do that? Vouch for me?! Huh? IT! WASN'T! ME!

> *(He has her backed against the wall, shaking. He then steps back,*
> *takes a deep breath.)*

Whoa. That felt really good. Was that a breakthrough? Is that what they call it or whatever? I'm sorry if I scared you—did I? Jesus, that was amazing! Well. I guess I should probably go. Thank you.

Hot Brown

Stephanie Caldwell

> Freestanding monologue
> Male
> 30-40s
> Seriocomic

David, a West Coast professor, pays a holiday visit to his family in Kentucky. When his "alternative" younger sister, Caryn, pulls him aside to complain about the small-town hicks she must suffer, he calls her out.

DAVID:

Well, what do you expect, Caryn? Seriously. What do you expect? You cannot dress the way you do, with beads and feathers and…are those bones?…in your hair, then complain that people on the street gawk at you. You can't get all offended and huffy if the person sitting next to you at the movies doesn't like the funk of your patchouli. You are purposefully and willfully and *deliberately* making yourself stand apart—no, stand *above*—all these poor, backward bumpkins in May's Creek, and then you complain when they notice. It's like some queen saying, "Stop looking at my crown!" Jesus.

Look: I'm sorry, honey. But…you can't be "colorful" *and* invisible in May's Creek. Trust me on this one. You're going to have to decide, and decide real soon, what it is you really are going for. You want to be noticed? Fine. Own it. You want to disappear? The piercings aren't helping with that. You need to get the hell out of here.

Is It Cold Enough For 'Ya?

Terence Duncan

>Freestanding monologue
>Male
>50s
>Seriocomic

New Rule: if you have a roof over your head, you have to earn the right to complain about the cold.

TERRY:

Over the past week, I've listened to many people complain about the cold. Yes. It was cold. But, it was not THAT cold. Low thirties / upper 20s is a great kind of cold this time of year.

Now, I'm not one to put people down. Instead, I will suggest a "Whine Guide" for Michigan Winters:

32 degrees and over: No complaint is justified. If you complain about this level of cold, you really need to think about relocating. This isn't Florida, for crying out loud.

31-20 degrees: No complaint is justified. If you complain about this level of cold, you really need to think about relocating. This is true, unless you are homeless. Then, you have something to complain about.

19-10 degrees: Only a quiet murmur under your breath is justified. That's it. No one wants to hear anything more. The homeless, however, can complain a great deal, because this level of cold can be dangerous.

9-0 degrees: You get one sentence (15 words max.) to voice your displeasure. That's it. The homeless, however, are facing a life and death struggle, so they are allowed to complain as much as they want.

Below 0: O.K., this is cold. However, you only get to use more than one sentence of complaint, if it stays this cold for three or more days in a row.

I know this will be hard for some of you. However, there is a loophole. If you go out and give your unused blankets and coats to the homeless (perhaps with some hot tea and food), you will be allowed to double your complaint quotient. Otherwise, you should just be thankful you have a warm car and house to which to retreat. Remember, it's only cold, if you're outside.

Little Airplanes of the Heart
Steve Feffer

> Play
> Male
> 55-ish
> Seriocomic

Uncle John, an overweight man in his mid-fifties, built an ultra-light airplane in a basement on Cape Cod, and attempted to fly it to Montana. He got as far as North Dakota, but in this dream play, Uncle John lives on. He sits in his airplane, and talks to his nephew, 12-year old Sam.

UNCLE JOHN:

I'm not sure you can understand this, Sam, and I'm almost embarrassed to say it, but when I'm in this plane, the feeling is very sexual. There's not much room between me and the engine, and it gives off the most remarkable vibrations. I once actually had a...a... very special feeling during the flight. The kind of feeling that I hope your father explained to you while he was alive, and if not, one that you'll find out about sooner or later in the schoolyard. It was right after takeoff. I don't think I was much out of Massachusetts. It didn't even have to do with sex. I felt so full of joy that I was flying toward my dream that it just took me by surprise. However, let me add that in no way did this contribute to the crash. I was not having...such a feeling at the time the old Volkswagen engine began to make the first sounds of trouble. (...) I never felt so alive. Even after the old Volkswagen engine sputtered out completely. I didn't think, oh, this was a mistake, John. You shouldn't have done this. I thought, Wow, I just really lived. I would like to live more like this. Unfortunately, I probably won't have the chance now. And then, of course, I thought, Damn, I wish I had lost that twenty pounds so I had room for a parachute.

Love's Labour's Lost

William Shakespeare

> Play
> Male
> 25+
> Seriocomic

Berowne bemoans falling in love with Rosaline.

BEROWNE:

And I, forsooth, in love! I, that have been love's whip;
A very beadle to a humorous sigh;
A critic, nay, a night-watch constable;
A domineering pedant o'er the boy;
Than whom no mortal so magnificent!
This whimpled, whining, purblind, wayward boy;
This senior-junior, giant-dwarf, Dan Cupid;
Regent of love-rhymes, lord of folded arms,
The anointed sovereign of sighs and groans,
Liege of all loiterers and malcontents,
Dread prince of plackets, king of codpieces,
Sole imperator and great general
Of trotting 'paritors:—O my little heart:—
And I to be a corporal of his field,
And wear his colours like a tumbler's hoop!
What, I! I love! I sue! I seek a wife!
A woman, that is like a German clock,
Still a-repairing, ever out of frame,
And never going aright, being a watch,
But being watch'd that it may still go right!
Nay, to be perjured, which is worst of all;
And, among three, to love the worst of all;
A wightly wanton with a velvet brow,
With two pitch-balls stuck in her face for eyes;
Ay, and by heaven, one that will do the deed
Though Argus were her eunuch and her guard:
And I to sigh for her! to watch for her!
To pray for her! Go to; it is a plague
That Cupid will impose for my neglect

Of his almighty dreadful little might.
Well, I will love, write, sigh, pray, sue and groan:
Some men must love my lady and some Joan.

Middletown (#1)
Will Eno

> Play
> Male
> 20s-30s
> Seriocomic

Middletown might be described as a Bizarro World response to Our Town. It might also be described as a ham sandwich, but that would be inaccurate. Here, the Mechanic talks to the town librarian about the space he occupies in the community.

MECHANIC:

(Moves downstage and stands very still, looking through the audience.) I'm nothing special, post-natally speaking. I fix cars, I try to. I get hassled by the cops, try to maintain a certain—I don't know—sobriety. Sometimes I volunteer at the hospital, dress up for the kids. It was part of a plea deal. But, what isn't. Nothing really crazy to report. Except. I found this rock once, everyone. What I thought was a meteorite. I brought the thing into the school, here. The kids ran it through all these tests, tapped on it, shined lights at it. I found it in a field. It looked special. Then the astronaut here told me it was just a rock. Said it was probably from, at some earlier time, another slightly larger rock. His name is Greg Something. I had ideas about getting famous, getting on local TV with my meteorite. When it turned out to just be a rock, I thought I could still make some headlines with it if I threw it off a bridge, hit some family in their car and killed everybody. But then I figured, you know what, forget it, that's not me. So now some family's driving around, not knowing how lucky they are, not knowing how sweet it all is. Just because. *(Very brief pause.)* Wait, hang on a second. Do you...*(Pause. He stays very still and listens intently.)* I thought I heard something. *(Listens again for a moment.)* I'm still not convinced I didn't. Weird. Anyway, that was just a little local story. Although, you know, it almost had outer space in it.

...People don't stop to think of how lucky they are. I do. And, I've realized, I'm not that lucky. But I get by. If I had more self-esteem, more stick-to-itiveness, I might have been a murderer. I was child once. Like everybody. Some worried mother's son or distant father's daughter, sneaking around with a dirty face and an idea. My hand was this big. *(With thumb and forefinger he indicates the size of an infant's hand. About an inch and a half.)* I was somebody's golden child, somebody's little hope. Now, I'm more just, you know, a local resident. Another earthling.

Middletown (#2)
Will Eno

> Play
> Male
> 30s-50s
> Seriocomic

The cop strolls through Middletown in "Our Town" fashion, talking into his two-way radio.

COP:

All units in the vicinity: see the man. See the man. See the woman. See the streets and houses, the shadows, the words that don't rhyme. All quiet here, over. No News is Good News, over. But there's no such thing as No News, over. Try to see my point. Just look at yourself, over. See the Universe. See a tiny person in the middle of it all, thrashing. See the bright side. Try to look at the bright side. *(Brief pause. To Audience.)* Sometimes I'll talk like this, over the wire. Just to see if anyone's listening.

...I do like this time of day: night. All the people. All their bones and arteries and personal problems. Beautiful animal: the Person. Dark. *(Pause.)* I was too rough with that guy, earlier. I think I embarrassed him. Regrettable. I'm not myself. Sad stuff at home and I haven't been sleeping, but, I guess we all have a story. Once upon a time. Once upon a time, and so on. The End. *(Brief pause.)* I try to uphold the law, keep some order around here, but I have my moods. I just remember screaming "Awe" at the poor guy. Hard word to scream. It just sounds like a sound. And you can't bully people into feeling something, anyway. Oh, well. *(Pause.)* We once almost had a Glass Museum, here. It would have been called the Middletown Glass Museum. Fact. *(Brief pause. He looks back toward the windows.)* Behold. You know, just, look...This is what life is like, here, right now. *(Brief pause.)* Looking in people's windows at night makes you feel lonely. Lonely, but, lonely along with the people in the windows. Along with the whole world, the whole lonely billions. It feels sort of holy, in some screwy way. Fact. *(Brief pause.)* Fact.

Middletown (#3)

Will Eno

> Play
> Male
> 40s-50s
> Seriocomic

In Middletown, the Male Doctor counsels pregnant Mrs. Swanson. Let's not confuse Middletown with Our Town. Or we could. It's been done before. It's just not a good direction to go in. Go left instead. Or right. Or what the heck. Confuse it with Our Town.

MALE DOCTOR:

Now, will the father be in the room with you?

Good. It's good to have someone. This is literally going to be the first day of the rest of your baby's life. Linguistically, you'll want to start him out small. Simple words like hi and juice and tree and bye-bye. Say whatever you feel. Most of it happens on a vibrational level, anyway.

...Love is all. It sounds so simple, I know, but, give him love. Without it, he'll just go around the world saying different things and seeing this and that and none of it'll make any difference. You've seen the type. Out in the rain, just kind of rattling around in their bodies. But, it's easy. This is the time for smiles and simple rhymes. Let's see you smile. *(MRS. SWANSON smiles. He barely smiles.)* Great. Wow. Did you see? You made me smile, too.

...His instinct is going to be to trust life. His actual animal instinct—I never get over this—is to hold your hand. He's in there, right now, listening, forming, waiting to hold your hand. Wow, huh? Neither science nor religion has yet undone the wonder of the crying baby in air and light grasping onto a finger.

...Don't forget—it's so easy to forget, but—everyone in the world was born. Try to name someone who wasn't? You can't. So just be a part of the whole crazy thing. The rest is details, little tests, taps of a tiny hammer. Oh, take one of these. *(He hands her a tiny white cotton hat.)* I get these free. Isn't it great? Did you ever see a tinier hat? Anyway, don't worry, why worry, come on, it's life. It's just good old life, been going on for years.

Middletown (#4)
Will Eno

> Play
> Male
> 30s
> Seriocomic

John Dodge tried to commit suicide. He attempts to explain himself to the Female Doctor who is, in fact, female and a doctor.

JOHN:

I know what you're thinking. I'm not this kind of person.

...I'm normally just a face in the crowd. In fact, I'm normally just home, by myself. Just a face in my house. Which is fine, normally.

...I didn't know what I was doing. It was like this cloud came over me, this big dark idea...That I wanted to be an emergency, somehow. I always felt like one, deep-down. I've got all these weird problems. I get nervous in certain weather. Sunlight reminds me of this great woman I knew. My heart races. I get these twitches in my elbow, my mind races. *(Brief pause.)* It always scared me there was even a word: Suicide. It scared me they even had a word for it. And then, suddenly, there I am. You know, on my kitchen floor, like a crazy person, right in the thick of that word.

...I pictured everybody with their eyes all red, saying funeral stuff like, "We hardly knew him." And, in reality, they kind of didn't. I never thought I'd have a lonely life. I do, it turns out. Like, medically lonely. Like I've got sad genes. Like, what's that word? *(Very brief pause.)* I don't know. I'm sure there is one.

...Please don't worry. I know I'm not crazy. I'm just sad. And not even that much, right now. I even feel hungry. That must be a good thing. *(Pause.)* I keep explaining, but—I wanted to see if I had a survival instinct. It was a stupid way to find out, but I did. And I'm glad. And I'm better, I think. Not fine, but better.

Much Ado About Nothing

William Shakespeare

> Play
> Male
> 25+
> Seriocomic

Earlier, Benedick vowed never to marry despite his attraction to Beatrice. Here, he drops his defenses for the first time and honestly contemplates his love.

BENEDICK:

Love me? Why, it must be requited. I hear how I am censured. They say I will bear myself proudly if I perceive the love come from her. They say too that she will rather die than give any sign of affection. I did never think to marry. I must not seem proud. They say the lady is fair. 'Tis a truth, I can bear them witness. And virtuous- 'tis so, I cannot reprove it. And wise, but for loving me. By my troth, it is no addition to her wit- nor no great argument of her folly, for I will be horribly in love with her. I may chance have some odd quirks and remnants of wit broken on me because I have railed so long against marriage; but doth not the appetite alter? A man loves the meat in his youth that he cannot endure in his age. No. The world must be peopled. When I said I would die a bachelor, I did not think I should live till I were married.

A Place to Crash
Martha Patterson

> Play
> Male
> 20s-30s
> Seriocomic

Ron visits a woman he hasn't seen in a while and believes he can win her over. He is seated on a love seat in her living room.

RON:

(Patting the seat next to him.) Sit next to me, Michelle. Don't worry, I'm not going to jump your bones.

Been five years since I've seen you. A long time. I think you gained weight. Thanks for letting me come over. *(Yawns.)* Sorry for yawning. Got high before I came over here. Made me feel better, since I just got evicted. Nowhere to sleep tonight. Hey! Let me show you some sandblasted masks I made of my face last month. *(Flips open his cell phone and scans through pictures.)* Experiments. I made them with plaster casts, then used plastic for the final product. I'm very artistic. I emulate the Masters. Rodin, Michelangelo *(Flips phone shut.)* That's enough of that. *(Looking around the room.)* This place isn't bad, but you could get rid of this funky love seat. And the bookcases. And that antique table with the TV on it. You could get cinder blocks, sell all this crap for money and live on the cheap. *(Looking her up and down.)* You know, you don't look like you did five years ago, but you've got skinny legs and you're all right. Face it, nobody looks that great after 30... Look, I was just hoping—*(He covers his mouth and yawns again.)* Sorry. No sleep last night. Hey! You hungry? I grow sprouts. Want to come out to my car and see the bean sprouts I have growing in the trunk? They're cheap—I eat for a buck a day. I studied food science in college. Interesting stuff. You could do a lot worse than me. *(Suddenly.)* So, Michelle—any chance I could spend the night?

The Political Insider

Joseph Paquette

> Freestanding monologue
> Male
> 25-40s
> Seriocomic

A man looks in a mirror and ties a necktie.

MAN:

Are you ready, Phil? You've rehearsed this speech for over a week. You've examined the dialogue and its message back and forth, inside and out. You've covered all possible, all plausible, philosophical, theoretical, hypothetical and pre-conceived conclusions, objections and degrees of error that may or may not transpire. You've considered every what if, could be and on the chance of, blah, blah, blah . . .

(Unties and reties necktie.)

You've mastered all required and compelling facial characteristics of a leader. The empathic mental agony expression. "You know I've been there." The gravely concerned look. "I'm here for you." The etched steadfast confidence stare. "I have the answer."

(Unsatisfied, he re-ties necktie.)

You've studied with the best of them, Phil. You've certainly have practiced beyond the limits of endurance and made their mannerisms—hand gestures, head and shoulder positions—your own.

(Frustrated, unties, stops fussing.)

Who are you kidding? Reporters scare the bejesus out of you. Nevertheless, the importance of a well-planned, well-run press conference is the key to staying in office and holding onto power. But the thought that a single rogue reporter may ask a question that has not been pre-approved and—WHAMMO—you're hanging out there like Nixon.

(Reties necktie.)

Let's face it Phil, a politician with a conscience is not a real politician. So you better get your act together because a lot of people on your team depend on you to keep them employed.

(Adjusts necktie, smiles.)

There you go, Senator, a perfect knot.

Pressure
G. William Zorn

Freestanding monologue
Male
40s-50s
Seriocomic

Walter answers a woman's question about married life with eloquence and metaphor.

WALTER:

Have you ever woken up from a really good night's sleep and when you get up, you notice something there on the mattress? Some change that fell out of your pocket, or a belt, or a racquet ball, I dunno. Something. Anyway, you start to wonder if that might have been why you had such a good night's sleep. I don't know how to explain it, but it's like it was pressing up against something that needed some tension, something pushing back against it to make it feel better. And you don't know how it got there or where it came from. I didn't, anyway. I sleep naked, always have. Where'd the change come from? And I dress in the bathroom, so a belt? And I could count the number of times I've played racquetball on one hand. But that was how it felt when we met. You're not listening. Big picture. Like something from out of nowhere, something you didn't even know you wanted or needed was just…there and it fit something in you. And it made you feel better for having made it through another night. Thing is though, you try to replicate it. You try to make it happen again, but it never works a second time. Because you're trying to make it happen. See you didn't know that the belt or the quarter or the ball was even there in the first place. It's like it knew right where you hurt and that's where it went. On its own. I…I'm not making any sense. It was the same with us. I think it's the same for a lot of married couples. You spend a lifetime trying to feel that…rested again. That free of pain. That complete and whole. And if you truly love him, if you are in it like the man says, "till death do you part," then when you are able to feel that way—and it does happen—you stay. Does that answer your question?

Smoker
David MacGregor

> Play
> Male
> 50s-60s
> Seriocomic

Uncle Lou defends himself by sharing his views on environmental friendliness.

UNCLE LOU:

Hold on a second! Are you saying I'm not environmentally friendly? How in the hell is it environmentally friendly if you gotta flush the toilet five or six times every other time you take a crap? You want to save water? Hell, if it's yellow, let it mellow. That's the way I roll. And you see that high-efficiency refrigerator? What makes it high efficiency? The compressor works twice as hard. What happens when a compressor works twice as hard? It breaks down twice as fast! What does that mean? It means a fridge that used to last fifteen years now lasts seven years and ends up in a landfill someplace! And God forbid anyone in this country should try and fix something! Oh no. Something breaks, you just drag it to the curb and buy yourself a new one. I swear to God, it breaks my heart when I drive down the street on trash day. Maybe that vacuum cleaner just needs a new switch. Maybe that lawn-mower just needs an overhaul. So when I see a beautiful, perfectly functional piece of art like this five-gallon flushing toilet sitting out in somebody's trash, you can bet your sweet ass I'm gonna stop and throw it in my truck. If I can't use it, somebody else can. And if it's broken, I can fix it. And if that's not being environmentally friendly, I don't know what the hell is!

Stars and Barmen
Reina Hardy

> Play
> Male
> 20s
> Seriocomic

Rupert, an astrophysics Ph.D. student, is at a party, hiding in a bathroom from the one woman in the universe he wants to avoid: Elaine.

RUPERT:

How big is the universe? How fucking big is the universe, is my question? In the bad old days of the nineteen nineties, some people thought that the universe might be finite but unbounded, a big sheet of space time curved around a gargantuan but theoretical beach ball, and that if you stood still enough, for long enough, and had a good enough telescope, you could see all the way around the beach ball to the back of your own head, and then you could jizz in your pants because you officially Knew It All. But in the heroic age of the early 2000s, we had a long hard look at the sky, and as it turns out, we know jack about it all, or at least, the size of it all. We know that it's expanding at 71 kilometers per second per megaparsec. We know that we can see about 93 billion light years of it. But as for how big it is, we only know that it's bigger than that. So my question is, given that the universe is either infinite, or really, really unfathomably big, how is that out of all the women in the universe that I could meet, at all the parties in the universe that I could crash, I would run into the one woman I know who is a dangerous fucking nut job?

Stars and Barmen (#2)

Reina Hardy

> Play
> Male
> 20s
> Seriocomic

Rupert, an astrophysics Ph.D., tried desperately to break out of his life in front of computer screens. He's been striking out. Here's a glimpse as to why...

RUPERT:

Hey. Wow. HEY. Great party. I feel out-dressed by the crudites. I am Rupert, by the way. I'm an astrophysicist. I'm in the business of identifying large, bright and interesting objects. I had to inspect you more closely. I'm not saying you're large. You're very proportionate. And shiny. It's fascinating. So I take it you're involved in earthquake relief? Cool. Excellent. Inspiring. Listen, I'd really love to take your picture. It's for sort of a project. A comparative survey of women I'm attracted to at parties. Yes, that does sound slightly strange. I can be slightly strange, fair enough. Would you like a candy cigarette? They're totally legal. Ok. L'Chaim! To Rebecca on the day of her womanhood. I mean, Rachel. Thank you! She looks very mature. Not that I care about that. I'm here for the older cousins, and maybe even some of the cool aunts. I am very open to cool aunts. They have all kinds of auntly experience...

(He stares at something large and unusual.) What is that? I mean, it's a 20-foot Pentakis dodecahedron made out of tinfoil, but what's it doing at a party? Is it trying to say "Listen, this party is way beyond you. You do not understand this party. You could be having a transcendent experience here if you weren't a total and complete imposter." Not that you look like an imposter, you look very appropriate. Appropriate, yet approachable. You have one of those faces. You know, one of those faces where probably crazy people just start conversations with you on the bus out of nowhere? Yeah. Well, it's been nice talking to you.

The Train Driver
Athol Fugard

> Play
> Male
> 30s
> Seriocomic

Roelf, a white South African train driver, ran over a woman and her baby on the train tracks and is haunted by them. He looks for their graves in a cemetery. Simon, the old African gravedigger tries to explain to Roelf that it is dangerous for him to be there. After much persuasion, Simon convinces Roelf to go with him to his desolate shack, where he will be safe. Roelf is stunned by the gravedigger's abject living conditions.

ROELF:

Ja well…as they say: no place like [home], hey? That's for sure. *(Shaking his head in disbelief)* If Lorraine—my wife—could see me now! She'd make me soak in Dettol for a week before she let me get into bed with her. God alone knows what she'd do with you, my friend. Because she's very fussy you know…'specially about bad smells and things like that. Hygiene! That's her hobby. Give her a can of Glade to spray around…you know… *(He demonstrates Lorraine spraying the air with an aerosol.)* Sssssss… Sssss…and she's a happy woman. Between me and you though I think she carries it a little bit too far. Like this dead woman I'm looking for…

(…) so I'm lying there in the bed in the dark, waiting for the pills to put me to sleep…and I was talking to myself, but softly, because I didn't want to wake up Lorraine…so I was talking to myself about all that happened and how it happened and about [the dead woman], because it just doesn't make sense you see, when the next thing I know is that Lorraine is sitting up in bed and shouting: "Will you please shut up about that bitch! This house already stinks from her! I can smell her everywhere!" How do you like that hey? She's never seen her but now she can suddenly smell her everywhere. Ja, home sweet home. I know all about it.

Use Storytelling on Your Product's Packaging to Connect with Your Consumer (#1)

Dan Kennedy

> Online magazine post
> Male
> 30+
> Seriocomic

This CEO experiments with a new way to sell new products.

CEO:

(Presenting the product.) HIDDEN WORLD ORGANIC ENERGY BARS.

We started making our organic energy bars for one simple reason: Our hate of the outside world. We were tired of people. Tired of their dented, damaged, and bereft spirit. Not all people, mind you. Not everyone is a bitter lonely blogger or Internet commenter stuck in their town and trying desperately to get attention and a ticket out by any means; the world hasn't rendered us quite so bitter and exhausted as to believe that to be the case. In fact, what little piece of us the hateful loners didn't take away remained aglow, and that's the energy we put into our bars. We did other things before the energy bars, you know. We made music and wrote, we painted, we did creative things like that. Broken people ruined them all. So then, why are our organic energy bars so vibrant and full of flavor? Quite simply, we are passionate about the idea of receding from the world and we think you can taste that. We love the flavor that comes from hiding out in a low slung ranch style house in an unremarkable suburb and selling packaged goods to people we'll never have to meet or speak to. As the owner and president of our little company, I was hoping the story of our organic energy bars would be a little more life affirming or colloquial. Alas, we were once spirited idealists who have been crushed into a fine powder of malaise and indifference, and all it took was years of enduring weak-willed lonely young men with Internet connections; precocious alcoholic boys who could use a piece of ass and a few of life's trials, to put it plainly.

Use Storytelling on Your Product's Packaging to Connect With Your Consumer (#2)

Dan Kennedy

Online magazine post
Male
30+
Seriocomic

This CEO experiments with a new way to sell new products.

CEO:

(Presenting the product.) FEELINGS® REVITALIZING BODY SCRUB.

Why make a evitalizing body scrub from all natural ingredients? Simple: We were going broke making energy bars. Hard to believe that one could find a way to make less money than writing books, making music, storytelling, and painting…but we did. As president and owner of our little organic company, I can tell you this: I was sick of my obscure and marginalized life in the arts, so I decided to make a simple organic energy bar that the world might actually hear about. I instantly learned one very important truth: there is, in fact, a way to have your name and face in magazines, newspapers, and on National Public Radio and make even less money than when you were being a creative type. With debt mounting and a rash of bad habits getting the upper hand, I knew it was time to feel renewed and revitalized. But how? Simple: I would create an organic scrub that would hopefully allow me to have a feeling of hope and renewal. As an alcoholic and addict, I am terrified of feelings. I'm not sure why I mention that, or where this little story is going, but I do know one thing: I need you to enjoy our energy bars and also our revitalizing body scrub.

Use Storytelling on Your Product's Packaging to Connect With Your Consumer (#3)

Dan Kennedy

Online magazine post
Male
30+
Seriocomic

This CEO experiments with a new way to sell new products.

CEO:

(Presenting the product.) PAPER SACK®.

The story of how our Paper Sack came to be is really quite simple. We set out to answer one little question that seemed to be getting asked with increased frequency around our very small living quarters/office: Where can you hide a gun when you don't have a car to ditch it in? Not long after posing that question barely aloud one night on the couch, Paper Sack was born. Paper Sack is a simple bag that is probably not organic. If you're like us, you'll want to keep several on hand! One to hide a gun, one to carry cash, one to write a note on, one to soak with gas. Hey, looks like I'm a goddamn poet again! Hey, looks like I'm wearing a mask and taking your money! It also looks like things are finally paying off for me. It's not like I ever asked for that much to begin with, so it's a shame that it's come to this. But as president and owner of a failed small organic foods company, and a former starving, albeit somewhat popular writer and creative type, I would like to take a moment to remind you that you had the chance to purchase plenty of things along that path that lead to me robbing you. But your story is that you chose not to. So now the story of our little organic business has taken a turn. A dark turn indeed, and we advise you not to struggle. Don't run or resist, we're under pressure and new to this, and there is so much that could go terribly wrong.

You Are What You Drive

Terence Duncan

> Freestanding monologue
> Male
> 50s
> Seriocomic

Reliable transportation is no small matter.

TERRY:

I got a new car recently. I love my new car. I love the way I feel when I drive my new car. When I park it, I always stroke the hood and look back longingly, as I walk away. I even gave her a name. I call her "Vinoa."

Isn't it something, how our senses of well-being and status are tied up in what we drive? I remember, after I was unceremoniously let go from Ford, I had to give up my Management Lease car. Since I had no idea how long it would take to get a new job, I decided to buy a very inexpensive 10-year-old, somewhat run-down, basic transportation. When I drove to meet someone I knew, I would park the car far away, so my friends wouldn't see what I was driving. It was sooooo hard to have self-confidence when I wasn't driving a nice car.

Besides, it was deceptively expensive to keep up. I could count on regularly forking out serious money for tires, brakes, belts, electronics, etc. It gets expensive to drive a cheap car.

Last week, I pulled up next to a young woman driving a late 1990s model, that looked like it was going to cave in upon itself. It was pouring smoke out the rear end. It had rust holes all over the place. The tires were bald. It was cold out and snowing and it didn't look like the defrosters were working. In the rear seat, were two toddlers, tucked in their car seats, in full winter gear.

Where was she going? What would happen if the car broke down? Did she have someone she could call? I have had trouble getting that young woman out of my mind. It's not because she was super-hot, either. Well, actually, I couldn't really tell if she was super-hot. I just imagined she was.

Where was I going with this? Oh, yeah. I was saying how thankful I am that I have a safe and reliable car to drive. I wish everyone did; even people who are not super good looking.

GENDER-NEUTRAL
MONOLOGUES

Declaration of Independence
Anne Flanagan

> Freestanding monologue
> Gender-neutral
> 26-40
> Comic

A therapy patient makes a clean break of it.

PATIENT:

So, today is my last therapy session.

No, I don't need "closure." I told you *four* sessions ago I was done and you said we should meet to explore my reasons for leaving, so we did and I said "Goodbye" and you said we should meet to explore how it felt saying "Goodbye" and when I said it felt pretty good, you said we should meet to address my "denial" and when I called you to say that was ridiculous you said we should meet in person to discuss why I felt the need to *call* rather than have a face to face so here I am and I am Not. Coming. Back.

I'm *done.*

No more affirmations. No more journaling. No more talking to an empty chair that's supposed to be my Father, who I never could really *see*, by the way, so I was faking that whole thing. I am done with Visualization. I am done with Meditation. I am done with chakras and chimes and crystals and I am so *fucking* done with Deepak Chopra, you wouldn't even believe! I came here to work on some typical, middle class family crap—so how the HELL did we get to chakras and crystals?! In the future, if I need help, I will join a support group or read the Bible or watch Oprah but I can Guaran-God damn-Tee you that I will NOT BE BACK.

But—can you still refill my Xanax script?

I'm Everyone on Facebook

Matt Ruby

> Freestanding monologue
> Gender-neutral
> Teen-50
> Comic

If Facebook could talk.

EVERYONE:

Hey! I'm everyone on Facebook. I'm grateful for how amazing this year was. I use a photo of my child as my profile picture. My identity is wrapped up 100% in this other human being and that is totally healthy. Kimye!!!! Gun control!!!!! Jay Z talking to an old lady on the subway!!!! Exclamation points!!!!!!

Here's what I'm listening to on Spotify. I have GOOD TASTE. Did you see that proposal where the guy hired a marching band? I cried! I bet that marriage will last FOREVER because the best way to show you truly love someone is to use them as a prop in your bid to make a video go viral since your improv group didn't really go anywhere. Watch this documentary on animal dictators. We NEED to do something about that issue I just forgot about. I don't understand economics but here's a link to a Paul Krugman editorial.

LOOK AT ME. At a wedding I went to. At a vacation I went on. At dinner. With my girls doing karaoke last night! I heart karaoke because it's like being a performer and people pay attention to you but you don't have to work hard or be talented. Afterward, we all commented on each other's photos: "You look gorgeous." "No, YOU look gorgeous." I just changed my status to IN A RELATIONSHIP. I hope people who rejected me in the past see that and feel bad. I am THE ONE THAT GOT AWAY. There is an icon of a heart next to my name now. That is the same as love.

I am OFFENDED by what someone said. Delta airlines lost my bag. I have OPINIONS about the news. This is my good side. Baby photo! Go local sports team! Beyoncé. The Elders of Zion are meeting at the Denver Airport. I just invited you to an event. Breaking Bad!! I find privacy settings confusing. I am a human being desperate for connection. Instagram wants to sell my photos to Al Qaeda.

I am SO grateful to you. I have edited out all the bad stuff from my life and presented the rest here. I am a Disney version of myself. Tag me! LIKE me! LIKE THIS! I'm worthwhile! Validate me, internet! VALIDATE ME! I am TRYING. Happy New Year!!!!!! COME TO MY SHOW!!!!!!!!!!!!!!!!

P.S. I forgot to mention: Someone famous DIED recently. I am SAD about this and this is my way of making it ALL ABOUT ME. (…)

Joy in the Heart

Pamela Hooks

> Freestanding monologue
> Gender-neutral
> 40+
> Comic

God is downsizing, and offloads some pithy stuff at a consignment store.

You know that book everybody's reading? About de-cluttering? The magical something or other of tidying up? The whole book can be boiled down to one sentence: "If it does not spark joy in your heart, toss it out." Well, this stuff no longer sparks joy in the heart of God. And my toss is your gain. Oh! Hahaha. You see what I did there?

Seems like the more space you have, the more you accumulate! Oh, sometimes I'll just set things outside the pearly gates— y'know, a footstool, old frames—some sinner or idolator always picks them up. But this time, I feel like this stuff really deserves to find a new home.

Like this: One pair of Jesus sandals, used. Lots of desert miles clocked on these babies, but still with some sole.

Three holy books. The Bible, The Talmud and The Koran. Never cracked. First editions.

What about this? The Shroud of Turin. I know what you're going to ask, and the answer is no. This is not the original. I've entrusted the real thing to the good folks at the Cathedral of Saint John the Baptist in Italy. This is a replica. But I should think it would fly off the shelf. What do you say?

I'm getting rid of ALL these "Jesus sightings," also. Here he is in a piece of toast. On a potato. A piece of bark. Soap. Tortilla. Can of Pringles. I've got a bunch with Mary, too.

Oh, and here's a great bunch of stuff. Check it out— all gifts from *guess who*: Fondue set. George Foreman Grill. Justin Bieber alarm clock. Zubaz. A Betamax. Did you guess?

Right—thanks Satan. Very funny. Asshole.

The Kindness of Enemies
Glenn Alterman

> Play
> Gender-neutral
> 17-25
> Comic

Invited back to the others' home after happy hour at a bar, this character is all over the place.

CHARACTER:
(Leaning in.) I could learn to love you, I could. And we could stay here, make this house, your house, my home. And you and me, we could have babies, *lots* and lots of babies; a big family. I bet...I bet you'd be a good parent. And we'd could get two dogs, puppies, any breed. And we'd move into a big house with a big mortgage! And if you're allergic to dogs, well some people are— then we could get *otters*. We can get like eight otters; have otters everywhere! We can sleep, drink, and eat with all our little otters. And we can name them. Names like Bim and Bam. Have birthday parties for each and every one of them! There'll be festivities and happiness in our home! And pretty soon, pretty soon, all our little otters will have *other* otters. It'll be OTTER PARADISE!—

So what do you think?

(No response. Sloughing it off.)

I was just playing with you. To be honest, I couldn't care less about otters. Actually I sometimes get otters mixed up with *weasels; dirty little weasels.* But y'know, most of the time, when I go out, for happy hour *(Looking right at the other.)* I can spot a weasel whenever I see one. Uh-huh, oh yeah, I can.

My Apartment: An Interpretive Dance in Three Parts
Pasha Malla

> Online magazine post
> Gender-neutral
> 20+
> Comic

A dancer creates.

DANCER:

Part One: The Landlord. Lights up. Immediately: greed. The hands are out, the belly is round. Smile. Step left, step back, step right, step forward. Squares. Now circles, like a vulture. Now turn, slowly. And freeze. Extend arms, as if for an embrace. Hold the potential tenant. Coddle him, stroke and swoon. Show the big bay windows, show the clawfoot tub. Big smiles. Agree to include heat and hydro. Twinkle toes, twinkle toes. Aren't you a friendly pixie? Shake hands and twirl, and curtsy. Sign the lease and twirl, and curtsy. Now freeze. Slowly turn again. Freeze. Take the tenant and bend him over, gently. Hold him from behind, prostrate, and begin to thrust from the hips. Be nice, at first, but gradually increase speed. Thrust, thrust, and what you didn't tell him is that the toilet runs all night and the neighbors raise pit bulls and only one of the baseboard heaters actually works and forget it if he thinks you're going to do anything about the broken lock on the back door, and smash the Tenancy Act with punching fists! Thrust and pump and punch. But. Wait. Big back arch, now… pause… gasp, and buck: the stinging scorpion. The body goes limp. Pull away, grinning. And jazz hands. And scene.

Phone-y
Steven D. Miller

Freestanding monologue
Gender-neutral
Teen+
Comic

A telephone speaks.

TELEPHONE:

(Making a ringing sound.) Ring! Ring! That's the only sound I make on my own. Everything else is just repeating whatever people say to me. In one hole and out another. It don't matter whether they're talking to someone or talking to themselves. Whatever they say, I repeat. It could be a hearty "hello, how are ya!" It could be a mumbled "I know I got another quarter here somewhere." But it's usually the same lame excuses—"I lost my cell;" "I'm out of juice." No one *wants* to use me anymore. It's just when they have to. "I left my cell at home; where did you say you are again?" "I'm here across 9th from Shorty's near 42nd like we agreed; where are you?" I miss the old days. To have an enclosed booth and a little privacy. Now I'm out here on the street like a vagrant stuck in one spot begging for coins. People pay me, and I listen to them. Half the time I feel like a psychiatrist and half the time like a two-bit hooker. People feeling me up to see if I've got a little something to offer them that the last patron didn't take. It's a dirty job sometimes, but I guess someone has to do it. I just don't know why that someone has to be me. *(Sighs.)* It ain't easy being a pay telephone in Hell's Kitchen.

The Successful Author's Morning Ritual

Brandon M. Crose

> Freestanding monologue
> Gender-neutral
> 20+
> Comic

Advice for writers.

SUCCESSFUL AUTHOR:

When you hear the alarm, do not shut it off. Do not tell yourself... that... you'll just do better tomorrow...*(Falls asleep.)* Reset. Alarm. When the alarm goes off, don't shut it off. Don't hit snooze. Especially
> *(hits it)*

don't
> *(hits it)*

hit it
> *(hits it)*

several
> *(hits it)*

times...
> *(Falls asleep.)*

Reset. Alarm.

Don't shut it off, don't hit snooze... Just get up! Don't check email or Facebook... Oh my god, she did what...?!

Reset. Alarm.

Just get up! Don't check the phone at all! Go directly to the computer.
> Don't check email. Don't... check Facebook... He he he...! Silly kittens.

Reset. Alarm.

Go directly to the computer. Disable internet! Open a Word doc. And... write.
> (*not writing*)

And... write!
> (*still not writing*)

Accept that writing is hard. Embrace the process.
> *(reaching for phone)*

Absolutely *do not* check internet things on your phone because it's right there and so, so much easier than writing...

Reset. Alarm.

Disable internet. Turn off the stupid phone. Engage with the blank page. Embrace the white oblivion. Rage against the void. Write something, anything. Anything at all! Write "poopy pants."

(Writes.)

Yessss. Poopy pants! You wrote those words. You will, I hope, delete them later, but that does not matter. This does: a moment ago you were just an aspiring writer, and now... You're an author.

(Getting ready for the day.)

Is that a swagger in your step? Why, I think it is! Good for you. Bask in that victorious glow—you've earned it.

(Energy begins to wane over the following.)

Just remember: Eat well today. Get some exercise. Don't stay out too late with friends. Spend tonight preparing for tomorrow. Get to bed by ten at the latest, and tomorrow...

(Crawls into bed.)

Reset. Alarm.

...Do it all over again.

Toward More Poetic Job Interviews (#1)
Dan Kennedy

> Online magazine post
> Gender-neutral
> 20+
> Comic

The applicant answers the question: "Why do you want to be a part of our team?"

APPLICANT:

Why do I want to be a part of your team?

I've wanted to be part of something for so long, there's this hole in me I try to hide, something I've jammed everything at; empty calories and half-hearted sex, travel and spending, starting and ending, any god's guarantees... Now, I ask you, what if all along it was as simple as joining this company to fill the part of me missing? What if some deranged wiring or disease has forced me to isolate myself away instead of considering being part of a team like the one here at your company? I feel pretty good right now, and I'm not even officially part of anything. Just even filling out this application is fixing me. How weird would it be if it turned out I don't even need the money, that I just need to be part of something, and I've idealized your team? That should be a movie. There's probably a Preston Sturges movie like that.

Toward More Poetic Job Interviews (#2)
Dan Kennedy

Online magazine post
Gender-neutral
20+
Comic

The applicant answers the question: "What are some of your strengths that you would bring to your work here?"

APPLICANT:

What are some of my strengths that I would bring to my work here?

A head on fire, a heart speeding through what days are left for me, a one hundred and forty beat per minute rocket ride back into the ether we all came from, and in the meantime longing to leave something behind, some kind of initials carved in wet cement, a stain on the planet, something proving I was here even just for the minute we get, you know what I mean? We look to leave a mark like a young drunk's bruise, we stare at our arms to see the boats our fathers fished on, drawings of what we touched littering our limbs, tattoos. Okay, so, picture the company a hundred years from now: imagine my work is left here somehow, even if the projects and meetings that I led are long gone, it's gone but my work is left here somehow, my strengths here in the muscle memory of these walls and desks and copiers and rooms—maybe some reports or memos or other documents I've typed are left in cabinets like ghosts in attics, dead flowers in the staff break room, thirty years later, come into bloom. Someone sees them and is like: "That's from a great energy that someone put into their work here. That's from a team member who was fucking extraordinary." Everyone getting coffee that morning is just quiet, like, "Yep, that's what that is."

Toward More Poetic Job Interviews (#3)

Dan Kennedy

> Online magazine post
> Gender-neutral
> 20+
> Comic

The applicant answers the question: "What was something you didn't like about the last company you worked for?"

APPLICANT:

What was something I didn't like about the last company I worked for?

If there's one sort of revenge fantasy I have about them it is this: I'm kind of on a stage or in a big field that looks lunar, like when you leave Ketchum for Boise. And I've dropped a little weight, and I start to scream and kind of sing, but it's kind of like reading or comedy, too. It's cool, I'm not explaining it well here, but I'm kind of scream-sing-talking like a '60s comedian or '90s punk singer, and it's lines like: "Why naynay naynah I can't manifest it! Baby, I! Can't! Float when they drag me down, your company to me, was like swimming in concrete! The whole department, coming on like cherry candy, winding up my deadly make believe! You hired me, played me, caught me, cooked me. I could've walked away but I was weightless, on fire; you had me! But my burn faded until your want was wheezing, your devour sated. Me, a frozen moment, hypothermic, one dumb bug there so still, waiting to thaw, goodbye millennium, been here so long it feels like I'm gone." Picture the guitar parts sounding pretty dissonant while I scream that stuff. I'm not going to compare it to other bands you or other people at the company know, because it would be my own thing.

Welcome to First-Year Composition (#1)
John Minichillo

> Online magazine post
> Gender-neutral
> 48
> Comic

This teacher of writing is a writer first, and a teacher second.

WRITER/TEACHER:

You may have noticed that there's a required textbook on the syllabus, and if you visited the university bookstore you saw there was a vast pile of them in direct proportion to those of you sitting here. If you bought one already, I applaud your ambition, but I'm going to ask you to please take it back. If you didn't buy the textbook yet, please don't. That is $80 you can use however you please. The line on the syllabus about the "required" textbook is for the director of composition, who isn't technically my boss, but he does exert his influence on us here and there, and it will make him happy to think we're using one of the textbooks he has reviewed and approved for us to buy and carry around. He's also the one who wrote the paragraphs on the syllabus that we'll be skipping over. He's an expert on classes like ours. So much so that he's fallen for the idea that a textbook is going to help you learn to write. I'm a writer and I know a lot of writers. None of us learned to write by using a textbook. No one ever did. In fact, if you think of yourself as a not-very-good writer, then reading about writing from a textbook is probably going to alienate you and make you feel even worse about writing. So we're not using one, but only because I'm not coming back next year and I no longer need to keep the director of composition happy.

Welcome to First-Year Composition (#2)

John Minichillo

> Online magazine post
> Gender-neutral
> 48
> Comic

This teacher of writing is a writer first, and a teacher second.

WRITER/TEACHER:

Since this is a first-year class, most of you are new to the university this fall. It's very exciting. You have profound personal and intellectual growth ahead of you. I've wasted my adult years teaching and writing, activities certified by schools like this one, paid for with government-sponsored debt, and I'm here to guide you.

Today, we're going over the syllabus as quickly as possible to acquaint you with what matters versus what appears on the document as teacher talk. I'm going to ask you to take a selfie on my iPad, which I will use to take attendance, and that way I can learn your faces. From where I'm standing there are too many faces. Your tuition keeps going up, I still make a laughable salary, yet they continue to cram more of you into my classes. (…) Not all of your teachers are treated with this level of indifference: not the celebrated ones you won't encounter until you've nearly graduated—they're paid quite well by any standard and they teach fewer classes with fewer of you in them—they also happen to be the people who have treated me, your humble contingent professor, more disrespectfully than anyone. Approach them with caution. You can learn a lot from them, but they will use your youth against you, and they need to be able to set the tone of every interaction. They know nothing about the murky job searches you'll be tossing yourselves into, which I'll be joining you in, though your prospects will be better than mine. I'll be forty-eight and I've only ever been a teacher. If I'm doing something other than waiting tables next year it will be thanks to some great cosmic accident and by no agency of my own. But enough about me, let's get down to some of the bare bones of our time here together.

Welcome to my Rare and Antiquarian eBook Shop

Eric Hague

Online magazine post
Gender-neutral
20+
Comic

In the world of eBooks, antiquarian is like, so yesterday.

EBOOKSELLER:

Why, hello there!—I was just appraising some rare PDFs in the back room when I heard you come in. (…) Please allow me—one of the world's foremost authorities on and purveyors of fine electronic books—to act as your steward through the wonderfully esoteric world of antique eBook collecting.

No, I'm sorry. The bathroom is for customers only.

But if I can draw your attention to our unsurpassed selection of priceless first-edition Kindle files, I'm sure you'll find something to tickle your fancy. Take this copy of *The Road* for instance: it was downloaded from Amazon only two hours after the novel first went on sale back in '07—yet note how the .azw file is still in pristine condition!

No, I don't have any DRM-cracked *Game of Thrones* files for Nook. Sir, need I remind you that this is a serious, scholarly establishment with an incredibly sophisticated clientele?

Wait, wait!—don't leave yet. For you see, you're not just standing in a cramped, unfurnished storefront in a crappy neighborhood, staring at a plastic bucket full of key-chain thumb drives—you're standing in the future. And if you can't appreciate that, well, then I don't want your business.

Ok, deal. Five bucks for the George R.R. Martin PDFs and the bathroom key is yours.

INDICES

MONOLOGUES BY AGE AND GENDER

FEMALE

Teen-20s

20+

20s-30s

30+

30s-40s

30s-50s

40+

40s-50s

50s-60s+

MALE

Teen-20s

20s-30s

20s-40s

Gender-Neutral

MONOLOGUES BY AUTHOR

222 MORE Comedy Monologues

CLASSIC MONOLOGUES

Permission Acknowledgements

7th Period Lunch or Someone's Gonna Snap Copyright by David Don Miller. Reprinted by permission of the author.

10 Ways to Survive the Zombie Apocalypse Copyright 2013 by Don Zolidis. All rights reserved. Reprinted by permission of Playscripts, Inc. To purchase acting editions of this play, or to obtain stock and amateur performance rights, you must contact: Playscripts, Inc. website: http://www.playscripts.com email: info@playscripts.com phone: 1-866-NEW-PLAY (639-7529).

After Copyright by Chad Beckim. Reprinted by permission of the author.

American Midget Copyright by Jonathan Yukich. Reprinted by permission of the author.

Annie Jump Copyright by Reina Hardy. Reprinted by permission of the author.

Bachelorette Copyright by Leslye Headland. Reprinted by permission of the author.

Bangs Copyright by Irene Ziegler. Reprinted by permission of the author.

Bereavement Group Copyright by Bara Swain. Reprinted by permission of the author.

The Big Day from *The Oberon Book of Comic Monologues for Women, Volume 2* © Katy Wix, 2015. By kind permission of Oberon Books Ltd.

The Big Hat Copyright by Martha Patterson. Reprinted by permission of the author.

Bite Me Copyright by Nina Mansfield. Reprinted by permission of the author.

Half Empty Copyright 2010 by David Rakoff. Reprinted by permission of the Rakoff estate and Irene Skolnick Literary Agency.

Bobby Wilson Can Eat His Own Face Copyright 2005 by Don Zolidis. All rights reserved. Reprinted by permission of Playscripts, Inc. To purchase acting editions of this play, or to obtain stock and amateur performance rights, you must contact: Playscripts, Inc. website: http://www.playscripts.com email: info@playscripts.com phone: 1-866-NEW-PLAY (639-7529).

The Bray of the Belles Copyright by David-Matthew Barnes. Reprinted by permission of the author.

Brogue Copyright by Duncan Pflaster. Reprinted by permission of the author.

Changelings Copyright by Reina Hardy. Reprinted by permission of the author.

Check Please Copyright 2003 by Jonathan Rand. Check Please: Take 3 Copyright 2008 by Jonathan Rand. All rights reserved. Reprinted by permission of Playscripts, Inc. To purchase acting editions of this play, or to obtain stock and amateur performance rights, you must contact: Playscripts, Inc. website: http://www.playscripts.com email: info@playscripts.com phone: 1-866-NEW-PLAY (639-7529).

Ching Chong Chinaman Copyright by Lauren Yee. Reprinted by permission of the author.

The Far-Flung Copyright by Julie McKee. Reprinted by permission of the author.

Flesh and the Desert Copyright by Carson Kreitzer. Reprinted by permission of the author.

Frank Amends Copyright by Halley Feiffer. Reprinted by permission of the author.

Friday Night is for Relaxing, Right? Sure it is. Copyright by Suzan Hyssen. Reprinted by permission of the author.

Full Plate Collection Copyright by Irene Ziegler. Reprinted by permission of the author.

Ghost of a Chance Copyright by Pamela Hooks. Reprinted by permission of Granville Circle Press.

God Only Knows Copyright by Michael Bailey. Reprinted by permission of the author.

Good Luck from *The Oberon Book of Comic Monologues for Women*, Volume 2 © Katy Wix, 2015. By kind permission of Oberon Books Ltd.

Goodbye Charles Copyright by Gabriel Davis. Reprinted by permission of the author.

The Gulf Copyright by Audrey Cefaly. Reprinted by permission of the author.

Havin' a Good Day Copyright by Terence Duncan. Reprinted by permission of the author.

Here's How my Humor Works Copyright by Patrick McKay. Reprinted by permission of the author.

High Grass Copyright by Irene Ziegler. Reprinted by permission of the author.

Honky Copyright by Greg Kalleres. Reprinted by permission of the author.

Hot Brown Copyright by Stephanie Caldwell. Reprinted by permission of Granville Circle Press.

Housekeeping Copyright by G. William Zorn. Reprinted by permission of the author.

How Water Behaves Copyright by Sherry Kramer. Reprinted by permission of the author.

I am Your Waitress Copyright by Kate Sederstrom. Reprinted by permission of the author.

I and You Copyright by Lauren Gunderson. Reprinted by permission of the author.

I Feel Like NPR Doesn't Like my New Radio Show Idea Copyright by Dan Kennedy. Reprinted by permission of the author.

I Think You Think I Love You Copyright by Kelly Younger. Reprinted by permission of the author.

I'm Everyone on Facebook Copyright by Matt Ruby. Reprinted by permission of the author.

In Which I Counsel Serena Williams About the Girls Copyright by Irene Ziegler. Reprinted by permission of the author.

Merry Cougar Christmas Copyright by Daniel Guyton. Reprinted by permission of the author.

A Meteorologist Works Out Some Personal Issues During His Forecast Copyright by Pete Reynolds. Reprinted by permission of the author.

Middletown Copyright by Will Eno. Reprinted by permission of the author.

Mill Town Girls Copyright by Audrey Cefaly. Reprinted by permission of the author.

The Money Shot Copyright by Neil LaBute. Reprinted by permission of the author.

The Monologue Show (from Hell) Copyright 2016 by Don Zolidis. All rights reserved. Reprinted by permission of Playscripts, Inc. To purchase acting editions of this play, or to obtain stock and amateur performance rights, you must contact: Playscripts, Inc. website: http://www.playscripts.com email: info@playscripts.com phone: 1-866-NEW-PLAY (639-7529).

A Mother's Love Copyright by Craig Pospisil. Reprinted by permission of the author.

Mr. Perfect Copyright @ 2015 by William Missouri Downs. All rights reserved. Reprinted by permission of Playscripts, Inc. To purchase acting editions of this play, or to obtain stock and amateur performance rights, you must contact: Playscripts, Inc. website: http://www.playscripts.com email: info@playscripts.com phone: 1-866-NEW-PLAY (639-7529)

Mr. Right Copyright by Jonathan Joy. Reprinted by permission of the author.

My Apartment: An Interpretative Dance in Three Parts Copyright by Pasha Malla. Reprinted by permission of the author.

My Carpet Liquidation Center Really is Going out of Business This Time Copyright by Patrick McKay. Reprinted by permission of the author.

Naomi in the Living Room Copyright 1991 by Christopher Durang. All rights reserved. Reprinted by permission of Helen Merrill LLC

New in the Motherhood Copyright by Lisa Loomer. Reprinted by permission of the author.

Nice Tie Copyright by Rich Orloff. Reprinted by permission of the author.

The Norwegians Copyright by C. Denby Swanson. Reprinted by permission of the author.

The Offer Copyright by Rand Higbee. Reprinted by permission of the author.

Out of the Water Copyright by Brooke Berman. Reprinted by permission of the author.

The Outrageous Adventures of Sheldon and Mrs. Levine Copyright by Sam Bobrick and Julie Stein. Reprinted by permission of the authors.

Paper Towels Copyright by Daniel Guyton. Reprinted by permission of the author.

Patience & Hannah Copyright by Gabrielle Sinclair. Reprinted by permission of the author.

Phone Arts Copyright by L.B. Hamilton. Reprinted by permission of the author.

Phone Conference Copyright by Michael Bailey. Reprinted by permission of the author.

Stay Copyright by David-Matthew Barnes. Reprinted by permission of the author.

The Successful Author's Morning Ritual Copyright by Brandon M. Crose. Reprinted by permission of the author.

That Bitch Brenda Stole my Lip Gloss (and I Want it Back) Copyright by David-Matthew Barnes. Reprinted by permission of the author.

This Will Not Look Good on my Resume Copyright by Jass Richards. Reprinted by permission of the author.

Three from *The Oberon Book of Comic Monologues for Women,* Volume 2 © Katy Wix, 2015. By kind permission of Oberon Books Ltd.

Toward More Poetic Job Interviews Copyright by Dan Kennedy. Reprinted by permission of the author.

The Train Driver from *The Train Driver and Other Plays by Athol Fugard.* Copyright © 2012 by Athol Fugard. Published by Theatre Communications Group. Used by permission of Theatre Communications Group.

The Trash Bag Tourist Copyright by Samuel Brett Williams. Reprinted by permission of the author.

The Unkempt Yard Copyright by Hal Corley. Reprinted by permission of the author.

Urine Trouble Now Copyright by Daniel Guyton. Reprinted by permission of the author.

Use Storytelling on your Product's Packaging to Connect with your Consumer Copyright by Dan Kennedy. Reprinted by permission of the author.

The Wedding Plan Copyright by Penny Jackson. Reprinted by permission of the author.

Welcome to Caleb's Humane Meats Copyright by Dan Kennedy. Reprinted by permission of the author.

Welcome to Christmas Village Copyright by Daniel Guyton. Reprinted by permission of the author.

Welcome to First-Year Composition Copyright by John Minichillo. Reprinted by permission of the author.

Welcome to my Rare and Antiquarian Ebook Shop Copyright by Eric Hague. Reprinted by permission of the author.

What Corbin Knew Copyright by Jeffrey Hatcher. Reprinted by permission of the author.

What Scares Me Copyright by Suzan Hyssen. Reprinted by permission of the author.

What the Terrible Psychic Said Copyright by Dan Kennedy. Reprinted by permission of the author.

When in Rome Copyright by Ben Verschoor. Reprinted by permission of the author.

Where's Julie? Copyright by Daniel Guyton. Reprinted by permission of the author.

Whore: A Kid's Play Copyright by Reese Thompson. Reprinted by permission of the author.

Special thanks to Carol Boynton at Smith and Kraus Publishers for so ably managing the permissions process.

EDITORS

IRENE ZIEGLER is an actor, teacher, playwright and co-editor of seven collections of monologues and plays. She lives in Richmond, VA and participates on many levels in the city's diverse theatrical community.

She also acts in films and TV, and teaches acting and playwriting. She was the original voice on your smart phone's GPS, and was once yelled at by Anne Bancroft.

ireneziegler.com
irenezieglervoiceovers.com

JOHN CAPECCI, a former communication and theatre arts professor, owns Capecci Communications (Minneapolis) where he is a consultant, story coach and writer. In addition to editing play and monologue collections, he is co-author of *Living Proof: Telling Your Story to Make a Difference*, a guide to using personal stories to advocate for change (with Tim Cage, Granville Circle Press). He has helped thousands of people from all walks of life use their personal stories and passions to make a difference in the lives of others and better the communities in which they live and work.

capeccicom.com
livingproofadvocacy.com